Going Local in Gran Canaria

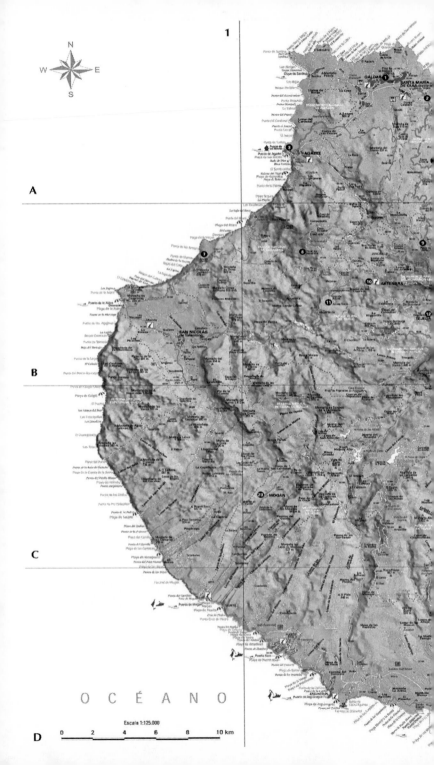

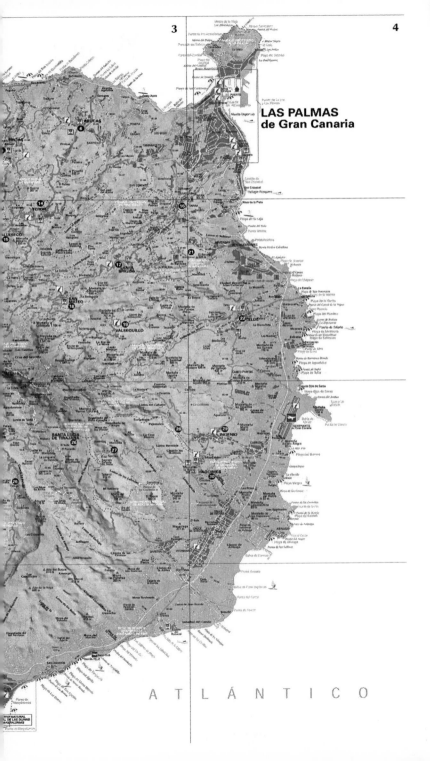

LAS PALMAS
de Gran Canaria

First Published Great Britain 2012
by Summertime Publishing

ISBN: 978-1-904881-62-9

Cover photos by Marcos De Rada Moniz

Book design by Creationbooth.com

Dedication

For Tom, looking forward to helping you discover

your very own treasure island.

Acknowledgements

If it wasn't for my wife Cristina, a native Canarian no less, I wouldn't be living on Gran Canaria. So I'm indebted to her for introducing me to an island I didn't know much about. Thanks also to my parents Chris and Hilary, brother Tim, sister-in-law Nuray and my sons Alex, Dani and Tom for being guinea pigs and, in some cases, taxi drivers in accompanying me or indeed ferrying me to parts of the island I hadn't yet visited.

A big shout out must go to photographer Marcos De Rada Moniz for the cover photographs, author shot and various other images of his home island. Also on the photo front, thanks to the folks at the Firgas, La Aldea de San Nicolás, San Bartolomé de Tirajana and Vega de San Mateo tourist information offices for their generous provision of said snaps. That's Fernando Toscano Benítez, Jose Luis Sosa, Pedro Aurelio Gasané Martín and Damián J. Ortega Gutiérrez. Last, and obviously by no means least, I'd like to recognize the contribution of Victor Manuel Sánchez Méndez whose weekly chats/English conversational classes have shown me yet another side to Gran Canaria.

Table of contents

Foreword

Research, research research – that's what I do whenever I visit any new place. I buy the relevant books or spend hours at my computer, ploughing through useless stuff, until I unearth a few helpful nuggets of information. I did copious amounts of research when Joe and I moved to Spain, stayed in America and Australia, and when we worked in the Middle East. How much easier it would have been if I'd had a guide like Matthew Hirtes's *Going Local* in my hands!

Going Local in Gran Canaria is not merely a guide, it's a comprehensive insider's take, warts and all. It begins with a very thorough overview covering just about every subject: history, culture, food and drink, transport, climate, economy and much more. There is a fascinating section entitled 'A Roof over your Head', in which Matthew discusses the options for those who may be considering relocating to Gran Canaria. To buy or not to buy? That is the question. And Matthew's advice is sound. He even provides links to recommended estate agents and lawyers, and explains what you will need to be granted a mortgage. And he doesn't stop there. Education, retirement, leisure activities and numerous other subjects are all dealt with frankly. Even nature lovers like me are catered for with suggestions of places we might wish to visit and what we may expect to see there.

Matthew has lived on Gran Canaria for eight years and draws on his wealth of knowledge to describe a host of towns and villages, discussing what each has to offer by way of beaches, accommodation, nightlife, fiestas and attractions. The descriptions are always lively and amusing. For instance, he comments that *Arinaga* beach is "windier than a baked-bean eater's constitution". This is what I enjoyed so much about *Going Local* – Matthew Hirtes's brutal honesty. If a place is unappealing, or the sun rarely shines in a certain spot, he'll say so. He's not afraid to voice his own opinions, which results in colourful reading.

I think I've visited every one of the Canary Islands except Gran Canaria. I now feel an irresistible urge to book a flight, with Matthew's *Going Local* clutched in my hot little hand, to discover the delights of Gran Canaria for myself.

Victoria Twead, author of:
Chickens, Mules and Two Old Fools,
Two Old Fools – Olé!
Mouth-Watering Spanish Recipes.

OVERVIEW

"Es una isla" Victor Manuel Sánchez Méndez explains the Canarian equivalent of "It's a small world", in this case "It's an island".

INTRODUCTION

Think Gran Canaria, think skyscraper hotels and eyesore '70s 'entertainment' complexes. Think again. From the ruggedly charming (in other words, warts-and-all) north coast, dotted with natural swimming pools, to the verdant and mountainous interior, Gran Canaria's so much more than your bog-standard package-tour destination. Peel back its veneer and there's a whole new world to discover. Which possibly explains why many of its 2 million+ annual visitors decide to return, some even to stay.

African in terms of geography but Spanish politically-speaking, you'll find Gran Canaria in the Atlantic Ocean, 130 miles (209km) off the coast of Africa. Cadiz, the nearest port on the Iberian penisula, lies 777 miles (1,250km) away. The third largest, despite its name, of the Canaries, the island's sandwiched between Tenerife in the west and Fuerteventura in the east. Las Palmas, located on the north-east tip of Gran Canaria, is its capital.

Located in the heart of the Canarian Archipelago, Gran Canaria's as round as a ball. And just as bouncy – with its inhabitants a particularly vivacious bunch. It may not be

1

the largest island in the Canaries but it houses almost half the population.

As any Hot-Spot theorist will tell you, the tectonic-plate splitting of South America from Africa formed the Canary Islands. A mantle plume expelled molten rock to the surface. Gran Canaria's origins date back 15 million years, but it wasn't until another mil had elapsed before anything happened above sea level.

The Moors once ruled mainland Spain, but the north African influence is as keenly felt on Canarian soil. Not least because of the shortish stretch of water separating the orphan Canaries from Mother Africa. They even import sand from the Sahara to furnish the dunes of Maspalomas, the jewel in the crown of Gran Canaria's beaches.

There are 80+ beaches on the islands. Chances are your average tourist will visit just two - Playa del Ingles and the neighbouring Maspalomas. Whilst this pretty pair are not without their merits, they're just the tip of, to extend the analogy even further, a whole north pole of icebergs.

Away from the main resorts, you'll find delights such as Sardina del Norte. When I heard an estate agent trumpeting this area as a 'zone of great potential', I thought to myself, *Oh, leave it alone, it's perfect.* An environmentalist acquaintance of mine, Cuco, is also worried about Sardina. He claims its tiny beach is unable to sustain the number of people who go there. And considering that these are almost exclusively Canarians from the north of the island, I feel slightly guilty even mentioning its name.

So, just as there's little grotty about neighbouring Lanzarote, Gran Canaria's not just an 18-30 mecca. Instead, to borrow a line from celebrated author Julia Donaldson, it's a land "with fiery mountains and golden sands". One which caters for outdoorsy types with a surfeit of cycling, hiking and mountain-climbing options.

Indeed, travelling to the centre of the island will fool any sat-nav into identifying your location as Asia with the mountains resembling a collection of mini Everests. For keen sightseers, it's an ideal destination with stunning vistas unfolding before your very eyes. There are *miradors*, viewing points, aplenty should you wish to pause for a more lingering look.

A World Biosphere Reserve, Gran Canaria's an eco-friendly destination. Around 50% of the island makes up this reserve, encompassing six rural towns with a population of over 18,000. Get back to nature on Gran Canaria with a stay in one of the *casas rurales*, rural houses converted into self-catering establishments and hotels for the benefit of environmental tourism.

The Canarian Network of Naturally Protected Areas, *Red Canaria de Espacios Naturales Protegidos*, is the body who looks after this half of Gran Canaria. Of the 146 protected sites under control of this network in the Canarian

Archipelago, a total of 33 are in Gran Canaria, making it the second most protected island of the Canaries.

Independent, but not to the extent of Catalonia, the locals seem as proud of their pre-Spanish past as their post-colonial one. Parents still use aboriginal names such as Aythami to christen their new-born babies. Although the Spanish World Cup win of 2010 was celebrated wildly, the reaction of my friend Tino was not untypical: "Bah, I'm African, not Spanish."

It's an island – views of Las Palmas from Gran Canaria's interior

"The credit crunch started on the islands when us Canarians stopped being shepherds." Satirical songwriter Arístides Moreno half-jokes between songs at WOMAD 2011.

A BRIEF HISTORY

Contrary to popular opinion, the Canary Islands don't owe their epithet to the real-life descendants of *Tweety Pie*. While these fluffy yellow birds are native to the islands, they were named after the Canaries rather than the other way around. Indeed, they were introduced to these shores by the victorious Spanish invasion force in the 15th century. Rather, the Canary Islands can thank one Juba II for their moniker. The King of Numidia and Mauretania, then Roman colonies, was astounded to discover packs of wild dogs roaming the islands on his expedition of c30BC. *Canis* means dog in Latin – which clears up the existence of the statues of giant dogs you'll see on the squares and streets of Las Palmas.

Juba II left the Canaries to their own devices, however. The original inhabitants, the *guanches*, which translates as man of Tenerife but is also used to describe those living on all the islands, were able to live in peace. It's generally accepted they were progeny of the Berbers. Although, given that these inhabitants of present-day Algeria, Morocco and Tunisia had no knowledge of ship-building, the question is how they arrived. The answer probably lies in the fact the emigrés were landlocked slaves exiled from their homeland by their Roman conquerors.

A life of isolation ended with the arrival of the Spanish in the 15th century. The *canarii*, the Gran Canarian *guanches*, put up one hell of a fight, though. Resisting for more than

50 years, conquering Gran Canaria cost Spain more men than in the conquest of the considerably-bigger Mexico. The island wasn't fully under Spanish control until as late as 1483.

Nine years later, in 1492 when Christopher Columbus sailed the ocean blue, Gran Canaria would serve as a stopover for the great explorer. The *Casa de Colón* in Las Palmas' Vegueta, actually the residence of the Spanish Governor of the time who invited Columbus to stay there as a guest, commemorates this occasion. You can learn more about Columbus' voyage at their museum.

Fast forward 444 years and another significant visitor arrived on the island – a certain Francisco Franco, soon-to-be-better known by his surname alone. Fearful of a coup, the then-Republican government transferred Franco to the Canary Islands. Given the nominal title of General Commandant of the Canaries, this didn't stop him co-ordinating the military revolt of July 17th 1936. The pro-Republican commander of the Las Palmas garrison dying as a result of cloak-and-dagger shenanigans kick-started the Spanish Civil War.

The Hotel Madrid in Las Palmas' *Plaza Cairasco* even put him up. If staying there, ask for Room 3, which is where he slept. Apart from the modernized bathroom and TV, it's in more or less the same condition as it was all those years ago.

Since then, Las Palmas has grown into the seventh largest city in the whole of Spain. Capital of the island as well as of the eastern Canaries, including Fuerteventura and Lanzarote, it's also one of the country's busiest ports. At the harbour, you'll see boats aplenty including both cruise and freight ships.

Canarians have a strange relationship with history. I remember, for example, when I proudly told my in-laws that my wife Cristina and I had just bought a house in the UK that was built in 1920. They couldn't have been less impressed. After all, these are people who purchase property like they buy cars. Something Giles Tremlett, *The Guardian*'s Madrid correspondent, in his excellent dissection of contemporary Spanish history, *Ghosts of Spain*, touches upon.

Tremlett homes in on this almost desperate thrust for modernity: "The *pueblo* is the old world. The city is the new. And, for most Spaniards, new is infinitely better than old. This is something that is obvious in a hundred small things – a virtual absence of second-hand shops, for instance, or the rarity of old cars. Nowhere is it more patent, however, than in architecture. Here great new things are being built and great old things are left to crumble."

It's a theme the *Guardian* man returns to: "The eagerness with which the new is embraced is something to do with the memory, real or inherited, of poverty. Again, there is an element of *huida*, of flight. Old, in many ways, still equals poor."

Yet, in the Canaries, there's been a bit of a recent backlash to this future-centric viewpoint. Where developers once paid scant regard to planning restrictions, now they adhere to them. Ecological tourism is also on the rise with rural houses and hotels an increasingly popular alternative to the full-board packages offered by the major resorts.

My own personal history of Gran Canaria came about following a chance mid-90s encounter in a nightclub. For it was at, in-their-eyes-only, "London's premier discoteque", Wardour Street's Vogue that a call of "What are you doing?" left me to literally drop the drunk friend I was helping to prop up. I replied, "I'm talking with you" to a tall, glamorous Canarian girl. In a whirlwind romance, a year later Cristina and I were man and wife. We married in the *Parroquia de la Inmaculada Concepción*, Tafira Alta's parish church to the accompaniment of a beautiful rendition of the traditional *Ave Maria*. 15 further years on, we're now living on the island, with our three sons Dani (11), Alex (8) and Tom (1).

Timeline

500BC – Gran Canaria's first settlers arrive, christening the island *Tamarán*, Land of the Brave.

1341 – King Afonso IV aka the Brave of Portugal orders the first maritime exploration of the Canaries. Three ships, led by Florence's Angiolino del Tegghia de Corbizzi and Niccoloso de Recco of Genoa, map 13 islands, including Gran Canaria, before returning to Lisbon. Later, Portugal would lay claim to the Canary Islands as if they were playing a game of Finders Keepers.

1351 – A papal decree establishes, signed by one Clement XI, Gran Canaria's second city Telde – making it the oldest metropolis of all the Canaries.

1451 – The first, of many, Englishmen to visit the south of the island – explorer Paul C Reilly attempts, but fails, to name the island *El Rondo*, the Circle.

1478 – As part of the conquest of Gran Canaria, a 650-strong force led by Castilian Juan Rejon found the city of Las Palmas, the future capital of the island.

1481 – During the Battle of Arucas, Spanish troops lance a boil otherwise known as *canarii* warrior Doramas. They later display his head on a stick in Las Palmas to deter the native population from further resistance. How very, very medieval.

1484 – *Agaldar*, *canarii* royal city by name and nature, falls into Spanish hands. With an imaginative reworking, the Spaniards drop the a and start to call it Gáldar.

1492 – In the naval equivalent of a pit stop, Christopher Columbus pulls into the port of Las Palmas to have his boat repaired.

1502 – An old friend returns as Columbus visits Maspalamos as possibly the south of the island's first tourist. As well as catching some rays, he stocks up on explorer essentials: firewood and water.

1595 – Locals repel seafaring hero in England's eyes, pirate in Spanish eyes, Sir Francis Drake, lured to Gran Canaria by the profits of the sugar-cane-export of the island. The *Fiestas en Honor de Nuestra Señora de La Luz* held annually in Las Palmas' La Isleta during October commemorate this victory.

1755 – A tidal wave from Lisbon becomes a tsunami, a buzz word back in the 18th century too, which creates the distinctive dunes of Maspalomas.

1891 – You can take an Englishman out of England but you can't take England out of an Englishman as expats prove in recreating the green and pleasant land by establishing the first-ever golf course in all of Spain on December 17th 1891 – *Real Club de Golf Las Palmas.*

1927 – Las Palmas de Gran Canaria 1 Santa Cruz de Tenerife 0 – LP takes over as capital of the Canaries.

1930 – King Alfonso XIII puts his autograph on a royal order, proclaiming the Bay of Gando military airport a civilian one.

1936 – Generalísimo Francisco Franco, Canarian exile, publishes his *Manifiesto de Las Palmas* on 18th July, calling on the Spanish population to unite if they love those old staples of brotherhood, freedom, and equality.

1956 – The bucket-and-spade brigade, all 54 of them, arrive in Gran Canaria with the landing of the very first charter flight.

1973 – Gran Canaria's population swells by 15,000 as those exiled by Franco to Western Sahara's El-Aaiñun return to Spanish shores following the death of the dictator.

1983 – The Canaries become two autonomous regions with Santa Cruz de Tenerife becoming capital of the Western Isles and Las Palmas de Gran Canaria capital of the Eastern Isles.

2007 – A disgruntled forest warden Juan Antonio Navarro sees his future career opportunities go up in smoke as he sets a third of Gran Canaria's forests, 86,000 hectares, alight – twisted firestarter.

In Your Face

I've lived in the Canaries for a while now but sometimes I feel very British. The British are generally reserved and don't shout. They say please and thank you, especially when ordering their beer, rather than banging on the bar top shouting "beer". Another example is the way they handle elections – or rather the way the Spanish do.

We recently had our local elections. About two weeks before voting day, we awoke to huge signs pinned to mountain sides, large banners erected and smaller pictures attached to every lamppost and tree. Each of the posters had a picture of the candidate. Either they've all got very good dentists or they'd been photoshopped. Their teeth looked great and I can tell you that as the teeth were at least a foot high in some cases. All very lovely but a bit disconcerting being watched by Paco Gonzalez (candidate for the PP).

In comparison, my memories of the UK elections are of the occasional quiet knock on the door by someone who has been roped in by their auntie's best friend who knows someone who is hoping to be the next parliamentary candidate. They stand on your doorstep and ask, very sheepishly, "How do you intend to vote?"

"Don't know," I usually reply.

"Ah okay, well here is a flyer detailing some of our policies," they say as they depart, shoving a small flyer in to your hand.

Here, I have no idea of the policies of each candidate. No flyers in my letterbox. I suppose I can go by who has had the better dental care. We have had cars driving by with annoying tannoys, terrible ice-cream-van tunes with a recorded message telling who they are and why they deserve your vote. These are like those messages you get at railway stations: "Garble garble train... can..." Mmmm was that cancelled or something else? This has been going on for the last two weeks and culminated in a drive-by of all the cars from one party, with all their tannoys and tooting horns and lots of balloons being flown out of car windows. They drive up the valley and can be heard for at least 10 minutes after they've left your part of the valley, only to return 20 minutes later – obviously after you've settled the kids down and told them that it's not a party, it's just some men in cars and no there won't be fireworks later (although there might).

By voting day, I still had no idea who was what. The white lines on the road had been repainted and the parks had been cleared a bit, obviously from a directive from the current party leader. The day after voting day, the signs are still up and I haven't a clue who's in, who's in by a hair's breadth, who lost, who's in jail and whose wife's brother's aunt is in trouble for not tooting loud enough.

Mary Beresford-Jones, British Medical Clinic nurse (www.britishmedicalclinic.com)

"The *guiri* (foreigner) cocked up again." Football team-mate Andrés, after another wayward pass results in a goal for the opposition.

PEOPLE AND THEIR QUIRKS

The racial make-up of Gran Canaria is evolving – and quicker than at any other time in its recent history. With increasing African migration to these shores, including intermarriage/co-habitation between Africans and Spaniards, the gene pool no longer looks so shallow. Traditionally, the inhabitants of Gran Canaria descended from the Spanish conquerors and the captured *canarii*, the aborigines who were overpowered by the 15th-century invasion force.

What's more, Las Palmas' status as a port of international standing has afforded it a long-standing cosmopolitanism.

There are well-established Chinese, Indian (going back five generations), and Korean communities (check out the Full Gospel Church in Altavista, www.fglpc.com). In the south of the island, many Germans and Scandinavians have made Gran Canaria their home, with Brits and Irish close behind in terms of numbers.

The original *canarii* are believed to have arrived on the shores of Gran Canaria, which they knew as *Tamaran*, between the 5th and 1st century BC. Rumoured to have been of Berber descent, this might explain why even today the average Canarian, especially the female of the species, towers over their rather more hobbit-like compatriots on the Spanish mainland.

21st-century Gran Canaria, with an average of 517 denizens per square kilometre, 'boasts' the highest housing density – not only within the Canaries but across the whole of Europe. Visit Las Palmas' rabbit-hutchesque La Isleta for further evidence. This has a lot to do with its statistically-higher growth rate, 3.17% compared to a national average of 0.29%. With the majority of the population aged between 15 and 45, Gran Canaria is also the youngest region of Spain.

Although around 98% of the islanders are Roman Catholic, they're less conservative than their compatriots on the Iberian Peninsula. There's a definite ambience of tolerance. Homosexuals in particular are known to favour Gran Canaria as a holiday destination because they feel less stigmatized here than in other locations. An attitude reflected in the gay-friendly laws which permit same-sex marriages. Puzzle at a chicken-or-egg-style conundrum when you discover former dictator Franco used to exile any soldiers found to be gay to Gran Canaria.

Just as on the mainland, Canarians breakfast, *desayunar*, like a pauper with a coffee ordinarily accompanying a doughnut or sandwich. They then lunch, *comer*, like a king, typically tucking into a three-course meal at home or out (known and sold as a *menú* at restaurants) usually from two o'clock to four o'clock with school canteens (*comedors*) offering a junior, earlier version for kids. Along with mid-morning and afternoon snacks, any excuse for another caffeine fix, there's not much room for a *cena*, dinner, which is often a one-course leftover from lunch and always a lighter meal than *comida*.

Siestas still exist, but more in theory than practice. Shops will close in the early afternoon but that's more to do with the long, late lunch rather than the local population enjoying a collective shuteye. Although August feels like one long siesta when anybody and everybody seems to shut up shop.

Mention dominoes and it conjures up images of old people's homes. However, while the players of Gran Canaria are not a great deal younger than than their British counterparts, they prefer an *alfresco* version of their favourite pastime. Walk through Las Palmas' bustling *Parque Santa Catalina* at any given hour, and you'll see tables full of old men vigorously, euphemistically-speaking, shaking their bones.

Despite the Iberian Peninsula being nearly 1,500 miles away, Canarians are definitely continental in their driving habits. The horn is used as an anger-release mechanism as much as a warning. Also, drivers will park absolutely anywhere – even risking a fine to do so. When the perfect parking space doesn't exist, they feel the need to invent it. Yet off the road, if the *canarios* were any more laidback, they'd be horizontal. The only arguments I have ever seen have been on the football field. Or off the pitch, and about football.

Three Men in a Boat – The Aldea de San Nicolás version

"So we have this seriously nosy neighbor. She's in her 70s, never married, and spies on on all of us that live around her. Case in point? One day last summer she actually screamed to us from the center floor of the building (an office that was being remodeled). She was either staring at the neighbors next door or eavesdropping on the conversation we were having in the kitchen. She wanted me to JUMP THE FREAKING ROOF, climb into her window, and open her door for her. She locked herself out spying." Canarygirl aka Nikki on taking the island's national sport of people-watching too far.

Bridging the Language Divide

The noise on our floor of the *cerveceria* is deafening. Note to self: must arrive earlier, in manner of Swiss person, when hosting own event. But this is Vegueta, in the north, where it would seem that the scheduled time is actually adhered to. A far cry from the soporific south. Unable to halt the chaos of competing voices, I find my student Stuart and hand him a fork. He gives his glass a forceful whack, and now they can see the tiny person laden down with dictionaries, because I'm standing on a chair.

Launching a national language exchange here has long been my dream, mostly because I'm fed up hearing that my students *"no tiene con quien practicar"*. How is this possible when Canarians and Brits live side by side and rely on one another economically? Plus, unemployment here is 25% and while the locals need English to improve their job prospects, few have the resources to pay for quality tuition.

I explain that to bridge the gap between us 'strangers' and the locals, we'll be alternating between Spanish and English in 15-minute sessions, accompanied by a spot of musical chairs. Looking around me, Las Palmas' participants are a world apart from the fish 'n' chippers that attend group events in the south. They're younger, predominantly professional, speak better English than I do and – oh shit, we are seriously short on Brits. In Playa del Inglés it's a different story: while foreign sun-worshipping language enthusiasts flock to *Café Florin*, most are gay, retired, or both, and in touristlandia the Canarians are thin on the ground. They´re either flirting at the beach, serving us lot *cervezas* or doing family time – the serious business of a lazy Sunday afternoon.

So I've learnt to bend with the breeze. In the north, I allocate one Brit to each table while in the south I spread my gold dust (actual Canarians!) as thinly as possible. Local people are gregarious, cheerful, astonishingly helpful and consistently tardy; just when you think the party's winding up, in they pour and up goes the decibel level.

My best outcome so far involves a shopless shop assistant finding work in a *perfumería* after I hooked her up with Steve for some one-to-one Spanglish.

"I just enter the store and say them that now I speak the English," confides Nuria, squeezing my hand. "You no pay the drinks. *Pago, yo.*"

The return on altruism is the warm glow of a full-bodied red. How I truly love this island.

Theresa Coe. To join the free language exchange, email <u>theresacoe@gmail.com</u>

LANGUAGE

Mind your language. While in the resorts, you'll be able to speak English and be understood. But venture out of these artificial enclaves, to the capital Las Palmas for example, and you'll find a potential barrier of misunderstanding. The only fluent English speakers you can seek out with any certainty will be at the tourist information offices or kiosks peppered throughout the city.

For those seeking their year-round place in the sun, learning Spanish's a must. You'll discover a wealth of academies and private teachers to choose from. A cheaper opportunity's the *intercambio* one. Here you meet up with a native in typically a bar/cafe. And over a *café* (coffee)/ *cerveza* (beer), you'll begin chatting in English for, say, 15 minutes, and then Spanish for the remainder of your drink or vice versa. Look out for the adverts on noticeboards in bookshops such as *Canary Books* (*Calle Senador Castillo Olivares* 51; 928 36 57 55; www.canarybooks.net). Alternatively, bilingual expat teacher Theresa Coe runs the *Gran Canaria Language Exchange*. Contact her on theresacoe@gmail.com – she'll then try and match you up with a native Spanish speaker in your area. Theresa also organizes monthly meetings if you're after more than one-on-one action.

Most Spanish who possess an understanding of a tongue other than their own will concede that grammatically English's an easier language to learn but phonetically their native idiom makes a lot more sense. If I could have a *euro* for every time my students tell me that English words are pronounced differently than they're spelt, I'd have already retired. What I always point out to them is that they're pronounced differently because they've been constructed with the English alphabet rather than the Spanish. We say A(y), they say A(h). There's a game kids play in the water with a beach ball where you have to spell out the vowels. My children quickly grow exasasperated with me because they think I'm monkeying about the order of A, E, I, O and U when I'm actually playing in English.

Cristina, my Canarian wife, can detect no difference when I say "ankle" or "uncle" in English. Likewise, one of her friends confused me no end when he told me he'd returned from a short break to London. What he was trying to convey to me was that he'd stayed in Peckham, what I initially understood was that he'd spent a night with David Beckham. Similarly, a nickname of a nephew of mine is *Pipo*. For a long time, I thought they were calling him Beepo.

At first, I couldn't distinguish between Spanish regional accents. Then a trainee teacher hailing from Madrid came to work at my school. While her impeccable English was decidely neutral, when she spoke in her mother tongue it didn't sound as if she'd just the one plum in her mouth but rather the whole tree. My sons still struggle to stop themselves cracking up when they're reunited with their capital-dwelling cousins during the holidays.

It goes without saying that the Canarians interpret the Castilian language rather more liberally. They run words together like Cockneys. But instead of dropping hs, which the whole population do (it's *(h)ola* rather than *hola*), they skip out the s's from the ends of words. So, it's initially impossible to tell if somebody hails from Las Palmas, the city, or La Palma the island.

If you learn one expression, make it "*¿qué pasó?*", a warm cross between the American "Wassup*?*" and Welsh "What's occurring*?*" It's infinitely more relaxed than the peninsular "*¿cómo estás?*", "How are you?" And even the informal "*¿qué tal?*", "How's it going?"

Carnaval Crazy

Armando was such a butch bloke – 6ft 3, a regular gym goer with a shaven head so shiny you could see your face in it – not the sort of guy you'd want to bump into in a dark alleyway. So you can imagine my surprise when he answered his apartment door dressed as a female flamenco dancer, complete with gigantic boobs, a full face of make-up and of course a flowing wig to cover his head-sized bald spot.

But this was carnival, where anything goes – including all inhibitions. And at least he'd made an effort. There's nothing creepier than a half-hearted drag act, yet you'll see plenty of guys who seem to want to take advantage of their annual opportunity to cross-dress and borrow their girlfriend's miniskirt but don't bother coupling it with lipstick, long locks or even a pair of outsized high heels.

Carnival in the Canaries is huge, with daytime parades closing city streets and night-time parties lasting until the sun is well and truly up. Dressed as a hula girl, a hippie, a clown and a moustachioed safari guide (carnival drag goes both ways) I joined with a quartet of carnival celebrations over the four years I lived in Las Palmas, sipping Tropical beer as the floats drove by and switching to Arehucas rum as the evening *mogollon* (street party) began.

The main event is not the crowning of the carnival queen, nor even the senior citizens' queen. It should come as no surprise that the headline event is the crowning of the drag queen. Managing to score tickets to the show in my third year on Gran Canaria, I enjoyed a live performance from The Village People (who else?) before watching 7-foot tall transvestites doing gymnastics in foot-high heels and feeling highly underdressed in my grass skirt and flip-flops.

Away from the arena, the action happens in the city's party park, Santa Catalina. Locals are festival mad and open-air events take place here throughout the year, thanks to the 'Eternal Spring' climate. Makeshift bars spring up for the duration of carnival, the rum flows, the Portaloos thankfully don't overflow and two weeks of mayhem culminates in an island-wide hangover on Carnival Tuesday (Shrove Tuesday).

The next day, revellers mourn the loss of their party for another year with a tongue-in-cheek parade culminating in the Burial of the Sardine (a huge cardboard fish filled with fireworks which is taken out to sea and essentially blown up). As the sardine is laid to rest, so too are the size-12 stilettos, the outsized dresses and the elaborate wigs – at least for another year as the city's part-time transvestites revert to their rather more mundane everyday lives.

Lucy Corne. Author of two guidebooks on the Canary Islands for Bradt and Dorling Kindersley, you can read more about Lucy at <u>www.lucycorne.com</u>

Unclouded Rock, Roque Nublo on a clear day

CULTURE

I'm not going to lie. Having had the pick of the world's greatest actors and musicians on my doorstep in London, the rather less-packed cultural calendar on Gran Canaria's something of a damp squib. Bob Dylan doesn't do Las Palmas. Neither do Coldplay. Although because of the Canaries' close ties with South America, the likes of Shakira do.

Although local politicians predictably got upset, unsurprisingly Las Palmas recently lost out to San Sebastián as the Spanish candidate for 2016's *European City of Culture*. And this despite the fact you could petition for LP three times from the same computer. Spain's culinary capital was always going to beat a city that inexplicably has a sightseeing bus tour.

The island falls rather flat on the museum front too. Though what they lack in quantity, they make up for in quality. Las Palmas' *Museo Elder de la Ciencia y la Tecnologica* (*Parque Santa Catalina S/N*; 828 01 18 28; www.museoelder.org) is a mini-me version of London's Science Museum. Located in Parque Santa Catalina, it's a popular venue for children's birthday parties. With 200+ interactive displays, big-screen cinema, planetarium and simulators, it's not difficult to see why. The *Museo Elder* proudly boasts a motto of "forbidden not to touch".

Elsewhere on Gran Canaria, *El Museo y Parque Arqueológico Cueva Pintada* (*Calle Audiencia* 2; 928 89

57 46; www.cuevapintada.com) in Gáldar is a must-stop-and-see on any visit to the north of the island. This Painted Cave Museum and Archaelogical Park offers a window into the lives and times of Gran Canaria's aboriginal ancestors. Don 3D glasses to catch a simulation of the early life of the *canarii*, the island's original aborigine inhabitants, and marvel at their beguilingly simple wall paintings on a guided tour available in English, French, German, and Spanish.

In terms of monuments, Las Palmas' *Catedral de Santa Ana* in olde-worlde Vegueta stands out. The Spanish started constructing it in 1500, soon after their invasion, and employed the Gothic architectural style. The consequent dramatic flourish ensures a high-wow factor, something the conniving Castilians had in mind – as they were keen to convert the natives to Christianity.

The conquerors can't claim another monument, *Roque Nublo*, as their own work, however. Clouded Rock is located at a height of 1,786m (5,859ft), and this conversation-stopper of a monolith was formed by a volcanic eruption around 4.5 million years ago. To be found close to the town of Tejeda in the heart of the island, it's well worth the trek.

You'll view plenty of artists in Las Palmas during the month-long mayhem of *Carnaval*. And the Spanish think the British have a problem relationship with alcohol? But if you prefer artists of the non-piss variety, head to the *Museo Néstor* (928 24 51 35; www.museonestor.com) in

Parque Doramas. Celebrating the life and works of Néstor Martin Fernandez de la Torre, one of Spain's most well-known symbolists and housed in the *Pueblo Canario*, Canarian Village, complex designed by Néstor's architect brother Miguel Fernandéz, this museum contains the major paintings of this maverick's maverick. Along with a comprehensive collection of drawings and sketches too.

Literary tourists should make a pitstop in Valsequillo. Here, they can check out the *El Colmenar* barracks, constructed in 1530. Of strategic military significance, these barracks also witnessed the birth of the father of Gran Canaria's most revered writer, Benito Pérez Galdós (1843-1920). The town itself houses a municipal library dedicated to this celebrated author, a Canarian version of Charles Dickens and Leonid Tolstoy rolled into one.

Visitors to Las Palmas can learn more about this writer schooled in the realist approach who specialized in books dripping with historical detail at the *Casa-Museo Peréz Galdós* (*Calle Cano* 6; 928 36 69 76; www.casamuseoperezgaldos.com). This house museum in which Peréz Galdós was born and lived until the end of his teens hosts a Galdosian International Congress every four years featuring a programme of courses and seminars covering the life and times of this writer.

Poetry fans need to travel further afield; to Moya and the *Casa-Museo Tomás Morales* (*Plaza de Tomás Morales S/N*; 928 62 02 17; www.tomasmorales.com). Morales (1884-1921), a cult modernist poet was born in this very same Moya house. Today, it's a free-to-enter museum which attempts to explain how Morales became one of poetry's great innovators. There are regular conferences, exhibitions and workshops organized with the goal of throwing even greater light on this shining star of Hispanic poetry.

Although they'll not feast as much as elsewhere, culture vultures won't go hungry on Gran Canaria. There are a number of theatres showing Spanish versions of popular international plays and musicals, with the likes of *We Will Rock You*, *The History Boys*, *Mamma Mia* and *Art* playing to packed, appreciative audiences. As well as performances of works by local favourites including Benito Pérez Galdos and playwrights from the mainland such as Lope de Vega.

You'll find the pick of the theatres on the island in Las Palmas. *Teatro Cuyás* (*Calle Viera y Clavijo S/N*; 928 43 21 80; www.teatrocuyas.com) offers 3,020 square metres of functional, yet funky, design and boasts a broad programme. Elsewhere, the beautifully-restored *Teatro Pérez Galdós* (*Plaza Stagno 1*; 928 43 38 05; www.teatroperezgaldos.es) and *Teatro Guiniguada* (*Calle de la Herrería 11*; 928 32 20 08; www.teatroguiniguada.es) put on regular shows.

FOOD AND DRINK

In the south, you're never far from the familiar waft of a fry-up. The resorts pander to tourists' home comforts. Which also explains the proliferation of Indian restaurants. By contrast, Indian restaurants are rather thinner on the ground in the capital, Las Palmas. Instead here the ethnic restaurant of choice is Chinese but as a teaching colleague of mine, thanks Ana, explained this has more to do with the fact Chinese restaurants are so reasonable than a love of edible China.

Although nothing tastes better than Mama's food, Canarians do like to eat out. A lot. So the restaurants aren't just for the tourists. Having said that, if you see more native diners in a venue than tourists, you can assume this is a restaurant steeped in authenticity. Either that or it's cheap. Canarians love a good grumble and none more so than after reluctantly paying for an expensive meal.

And in these credit-crunch times, the traditional Spanish *menú* has never been so popular. At lunchtimes, most restaurants will offer a set menu, comprising two to three starters, the same number of main courses, and three to five desserts. While these tend to be meat- or fish-based, you're usually able to arrange vegetarian alternatives.

Generally though, the Canarians are massive fans of Spanish cuisine. *Paella*, a filling rice dish, and *tortilla* (Spanish omelette which is nothing like the English version but typically a doorstep-thick omelette bulked up with copious onion and potato) are as popular here as on the mainland. As is *chorizo*, the sweet-yet-garlickly sausage which infamously repeats on you. Kids here love to gross out their classmates with fearsome chorizo burps.

Being an island, fish is a staple, in particular tuna. Which appears in a multitude of dishes. For example, at my local fast-food takeaway, they serve hot dogs with tuna and eggs on top. And as a vegetarian, I have learned (the hard way) to always ask for an *ensalada mixta* (mixed salad) *sin atun* (without tuna).

Instead of *patatas bravas* (fried potatoes served with a fiery sauce), you'll find *papas arrugadas*, baby wrinkled potatoes cooked in plenty of salty water, accompanied by *mojo* – a sauce which can be orange, red, or green and either mild or spicy depending on the ingredients used. *Mojo* usually comprises a combination of olive oil, vinegar, paprika, thyme, oregano and coriander. I've sampled *mojo* which wouldn't look out of place on a Tandoori restaurant menu along with some I'd swear was actually barbecue sauce.

Another quintessentially Canarian foodstuff is *gofio*, a flour created by grinding roasted grains (typically barley, corn, or wheat). The base of a mousse or ice-cream, it's also used to make *gofio escaldado*, with the flour mixed in with boiling fish stock to create a dip-cum-scoop you eat/shovel accompanied by slices of red onion. Then's there *ropa vieja*, old clothes, which is more appetizing than it sounds – made of chicken and beef combined with garlic, onion, potatoes, chickpeas, pepper, tomato and white wine.

The wine from the *Malvasia* grape was raved about by no less a figure than Shakespeare. Gran Canaria lags a little behind Lanzarote and Tenerife in terms of production and quality, but vineyards here are slowly but surely garnering a good reputation amongst wine critics. Gran Canaria wines tend to be full-bloodied reds or dry whites and are usually exclusively produced for the Canarian market alone, given the low number of vineyards on the island.

I can barely recall my first *cubata*. It was my first trip to Las Palmas. My theory is that you get to know a city through its nightlife. So I ventured out of the hostel I was staying in. And found a bar. In a mishmash of Spanglish and sign language, I ordered a rum and Coke. Except the rum was served in a tall glass and the barman kept pouring, until it was over half full. It was later pointed out to me that at certain venues they expect you to tell them when you want them to stop pouring. As you might imagine, I have no recollection of how I made it back to my accommodation that night.

As I've later discovered, the secret to a perfect *cubata* is the lemon. If you're preparing it yourself, cut the fruit in half and gently squeeze it around the rim. For a lesser effect, there's always a slice to accompany the ice. The bitterness of the lemon is crucial, however, to counteract the sweet rum (main ingredient: sugar cane) and Coke (main ingredient: sugar).

I favour *Arehucas Carta Oro* but football teammates have tried to convince me to switch to *Telde Blanco* as it apparently contains fewer chemicals and therefore doesn't result in a hangover. I've heard this argument before. Prior to travelling to study in the Czech Republic I'd been assured that the beer there was so pure, you'd avoid the fuzzy morning-after-the-night-before feeling students view as a ritual. A theory that myself and my fellow alumni disproved. Time and time again.

Shank's Pony favours the descent over the ascent

TRANSPORT

Although their location would suggest otherwise, the Canaries are part of Spain. And therefore a member of the European Union. Usual travel regulations apply. You'll only be allowed entry if you're in possession of a valid passport or identity card – the latter an official Spanish form of identification which enables Iberian residents to travel without a passport.

Nationals of some specified countries will also require a visa – particularly if a long-term stay is planned. If you're at all uncertain, we recommend contacting your travel agency or the Embassy/Consulate of Spain where you live – before embarking upon your journey.

You'll be able to pick up a scheduled flight from and to any other Canary Island plus numerous airports on the Peninsula itself. Most major European cities also run charter flights to Gran Canaria (formerly Gando) airport. Bear in mind, however, the airport code is LPA (short for Las Palmas).

There are three main ferry companies servicing Gran Canaria, running ferries to other Canary Islands and beyond. You can book a ferry ticket with *Fred. Olsen, S.A.* (902 10 01 07; www.fredolsen.es), from Agaete to El Hierro's Valverde, San Sebastian de La Gomera, Santa Cruz de La Palma, and Santa Cruz de Tenerife, and from Las Palmas to Arrecife on Lanzarote and Fuerteventura's Puerto del Rosario. *Naviera Armas* (902 45 65 00;

www.navieraarmas.com), meanwhile, offer ferries to the same destinations, along with Fuerteventura's Gran Tarajal and Morrajable. They also provide services to Maderia's Funchal and Portimao on the Portuguese mainland. All their ferries depart from Las Palmas.

Acciona Trasmeditteránea (902 45 46 45; www.trasmediterranea.es) specialize in ferries from and to the Balearics, Canaries and the Straits of Gibraltar. You can book single or return tickets online. Their destinations travelling from Las Palmas number Arrecife, Barcelona, Cadiz, Puerto del Rosario, Santa Cruz de La Palma, Santa Cruz de Tenerife, and Seville.

With a surface area of just 1,500 square kms (590 square miles), Gran Canaria's relatively easy to tranverse. With an established tourist infrastructure too, it boasts an excellent transport system. However, the geographical layout of the island, including a mountainous centre and rocky coastline, means navigating Gran Canaria isn't quite as simple as you first assumed.

There are no trains on the island. A route linking the capital, Las Palmas, in the north of the island and the resorts in the south, going as far as Maspalomas, has long been mooted. But the ongoing credit crunch seems to have put any further rail-related discussions on hold.

However, there's a regular bus service connecting the airport with both Las Palmas in the north and the major resorts in the south. In Las Palmas you can travel almost anywhere you want to on the yellow *Guaguas Municipales* (902 07 77 78; www.guaguas.com), city buses. By buying a *bono de guagua*, bus pass, available in most newsagents on your arrival in the city, you'll be able to save around 50 per cent on your bus journeys. But be warned that the services are severely reduced over the weekends and on public holidays.

You can pick up a *tarjeta insular*, multi-journey ticket, for the blue *Global* (928 25 26 30; www.globalsu.net) buses which link locations across the island too. These are usually only available at bus stations. Even buying a return in advance rather than paying on board can save you money too. For example, if you buy a return from the window to the south from Las Palmas they will charge you €6.50, a *euro* cheaper than the single they will charge you on board. The *Global* buses travel to the smallest *pueblo* (village) but be warned that you're going to have to navigate some winding, nausea-inviting, roads along the way.

Similarly driving in the mountainous areas can be arduous with spiral roads and hairpin bends a test for even the most experienced drivers, so allow plenty of time for your journey. It's also a good idea to have a paper or plastic bag to hand, should one of your passengers succumb to one of the more explosive symptoms of carsickness – on a recent two-hour journey from our home to the island's interior my wife had to stop five times to clear up kiddie vomit. Be advised that the only fast roads on the island are the GC-1 motorway linking Las Palmas with Arguineguín and the GC-2, connecting Agaete with the capital.

Señor Blue Sky

We were attracted to Gran Canaria by the climate and although I'm not a great fan of the beach I do like to wake up to a blue sky and sunshine. Of course, for beach and water sports GC is hard to beat. The tourist board is actively promoting a variety of events, the number of which seems to increase each year and tend to be very well organized. During the year there are several important walking and cycling events that take place.

The main advantage living here, apart from the benefit of year-round sunshine, is that everything seems to cost less. Apart from the obvious items like drink and petrol, my subsidized pilates class costs only 4 Euros a month and there are a variety of classes to choose from. Numerous parks and jogging tracks have sprung up in recent times. A major comparison with the UK is that our rates are a lot cheaper and the services we receive a lot better. Here our rubbish is collected almost daily and we have a sensible and easy way to recycle.

Our experience of the Spanish National Health Service, the *Sistema Nacional de Salud* (*SNS*) has been excellent and repeat prescriptions are now computerized as is the whole system. My husband broke his hip and choose the NHS over private as the Las Palmas Dr Negrin hospital is reputed to be state of the art. He was certainly very impressed with everything including the food, cleanliness and speed, in four days he was up and 'running'.

Another advantage is the size of the island. Nothing is too far away. Unlike the UK where one can spend five hours in the traffic on a bank holiday! So here we intend to stay and work on a project in the mountains, which is intended to be a haven or refuge and an ideal place for green and eco-friendly tourism. The house is in the mountains, above Gáldar, and is surrounded by fields. The land around it will be planted in permaculture style and domestic water will be reused to irrigate the fruit trees. It will be an ideal place for walkers and rural tourists to stay over night or for longer periods. The plan includes a yurt for meditation and/or therapies and courses.

The *finca* should be self-sufficient in fruit, vegetables, eggs and honey and there will be an herb garden. It will also be promoted as an EMF- and microwave-free house as there will be the option to choose not to use the generated electric power and to use oil lamps and manual gadgets instead! It will cater for a growing number of people who are affected by mobile-phone antennas and high-power electric cables in their home vicinity and wish to give their bodies a break and a healthy few days holiday away from all that e-smog!

Sheena Gallagher. For more information on all this and properties for sale all over Gran Canaria visit www.canary-property.com

Wetter than you think

CLIMATE

Not for nothing is Gran Canaria known as a mini continent. Generally, the south is hotter than the north and the west clearer than the east. But things are a little bit topsy turvy, particularly in the capital Las Palmas which arguably enjoys a sunnier winter than summer.

Nevertheless, Thomas Whitmore, director of research on climatology at Syracuse University, concludes in a 1996 scientific study entitled *Pleasant Weather Ratings* that the city enjoys "the best climate in the world" compared to 599 other metropolises. Yet Las Palmas shares the dubious distinction of being the city with the best weather in the world but the worst on the island. Vecindario perhaps rivals LP here, resembling an elderly relative in that it suffers from problem wind. To the extent that its palm trees don't stand straight but bend eastwards.

Once my brother came to visit us in August and stayed at my mother-in-law's apartment overlooking *Canteras* beach. Summer's the season of the *panza de burro*, donkey's belly, a big black cloud which envelops the city, keeping the temperature down by blocking out the sun. "Nobody's going to believe I've been on holiday," he whinged.

Gran Canaria's the land of microclimates. Once we were lunching with my parents in El Roque on the north coast. As we were finishing, the clouds came out and it started to rain. My sons thought our plans for an afternoon trip to the beach had been well and truly scuppered. "Don't worry, it'll be sunny in Sardina," I claimed. Sardina del Norte was a mere 10 minutes away by car. 10 minutes later, we're slapping on the sun cream and hitting the beach – perhaps crucially because it's west of El Roque and not east, and further away than rather than closer to Las Palmas.

The island's average annual temperatures peak at 25 and dip no lower than 18. It's generally chilled without being chilly and Madras rather than Vindaloo-hot. Although the higher you go on Gran Canaria, the more the temperature falls – with the summits of the mountains dropping as low as 0 degrees.

January Avg precip: ....**1.46 cm**
February Avg precip: ....**1.81 cm**
March Avg precip: ....**1.17 cm**
April Avg precip: ....**0.29 cm**
May Avg precip: ....**0.07 cm**
June Avg precip: ....**0.09 cm**
July Avg precip: ....**0.09 cm**
August Avg precip: ....**0.06 cm**
September Avg precip: ......**0.35 cm**
October Avg precip: ....**1.07 cm**
November Avg precip: ......**1.56 cm**
December Avg precip: ....**2.5 cm**

Sunshine hours

January 6
February 6
March 7
April 8
May 8
June 9
July 10
August 9
September 8
October 7
November 6
December 5

"*Cuñado,* you look like a lobster." My decision to wear a lower-factor sun cream in order to emulate the golden brown of your average Canarian backfires as brother-in-law Jorgé gleefully points out.

Seasons in the sun, spring and summer rolled into one

ECONOMY

A German, an Englishman, an Irishman and a Canarian enter a Playa del Inglés bar. The German pays for the drinks. Unfortunately, the credit crunch's no laughing matter. It's hit local businesses hard. The unemployment rate on the island has dropped as low (or is that as high?) as 25%.

Before the bust there was the boom with new housing springing up just about everywhere. Many of these new developments apparently lie dormant. On the flip side, there are property bargains to be had as it's definitely a buyer's market at the moment. There isn't a better time than now to purchase your place in the sun. Although there are many Canarians who are content to sit on their property and wait for the economy to pick up in order for their asking price to be met.

Those looking for work in the south can generally find casual shifts in the expat bars, especially if you don't speak Spanish but bear in mind these tend to drop off in the winter when the island attracts more German and Scandinavian tourists. Part-time tour operator positions are thin on the ground but it's worthwhile contacting the likes of Thomas Cook when you're over here as they might need a hand with an airport run or excursion. It's harder to come by temping positions in the north and you can forget landing bar, hospital, or restaurant work if you don't speak fluent Spanish.

"*Mójate!* Scantily clad chicks and blokes (unfortunately) having a dance off on two pedestals over a pool. The loser gets thrown into the pool. 50-minute show, 4 nights a week – who says the Spanish don't make quality TV?" Fellow teacher Joe Mannion critiques Spanish television

Suburbs Gran Canaria Style

A ROOF OVER YOUR HEAD

To buy or not to buy? It's a question mulled over by property-seekers no matter where they're searching. With the European economy still unstable, you'd think there'd be bargains to be had on Gran Canaria. And you'd be right – to an extent. While prices have gone down, properties which were for sale pre-bust remain for sale. Either the seller has enough money to wait until what they consider a fair offer is matched or the seller can't afford to let their property go at a lower price.

Renting therefore remains a popular option. It's also a way to ease yourself into the Canarian property market. If you are relocating without knowing the island, something to be avoided if you can, it's worth taking a short-term rent as a way to get acquainted with an area. For example, you might've already come to the conclusion you prefer the home comforts of the south where your neighbour's more likely than not to be an expat. Until you settle there and find out you prefer the more going-native-friendly north where you won't find an English-language newspaper at every kiosk nor English breakfast at every cafe.

Another option, especially if you're relocating alone, is to share a property. Check out the local press for adverts. You'll also find ads in Las Palmas's English-language bookshops, *Canary Books* (*Calle Senador Castillo Olivares* 51; 928 36 57 55; www.canarybooks.net) and *Idiomatika* (*Calle Senador Castillo Olivares* 52; 928 43 32 65; www.idiomatika.net). As well as displayed on random lampposts.

More extreme options include renovating an old property. But beware the red tape. Everybody blames Franco for the bureaucracy-crazy Spanish society. Whoever's culpable, expect to spend plenty of time visiting various government buildings where various pieces of paper will have to be stamped by various departments. Remember to bring proof of identity with you. The authorities get off on asking you for this and will point-blank refuse to deal with you if you're missing any documentation, send you on your sorry way with not so much as a smile, and then you'll have to repeat the whole torturous process.

Yet another alternative's to buy land and then build your own property. This is definitely the cheaper option.

However, the whole procedure's fraught with more pitfalls than *Indiana Jones* typically has to face. Spanish land laws are as intricate as a labyrinth and just as difficult to navigate.

Most estate agents will have at least one English- or German-speaking member of staff on their books. The family-run *Canary Property Market* (*Calle El Calvario* 16, San Lorenzo; 928 67 17 31; www.canary-property. com) has been advising property-seekers since 1972 and the firm's Sheena Gallagher is a font of reassurance for first-time buyers in this region. Also worth contacting are *Cardenas* (*Calle La Lajilla* 2, Arguineguín; 928 15 06 50; www.cardenas-grancanaria.com) who boast offices in *Playa Mogan* and *Puerto Rico* as well, and *Südland* (*Calle Juan Manuel Duran* 25, Las Palmas; 928 26 08 06; www.suedland.com).

Whatever your property needs, you're also going to require the services of an *abogado* (lawyer). If looking to live in Las Palmas or elsewhere in the north of the island your best bet's to contact *OGMA* (Calle Cebrián 27; 928 38 43 92) who look after English, German and indeed Spanish clients. With a similarly international customer base, *Rivero y Mendoza Abogados* (Avenída Tirajana 39; 928 73 01 61) are the go-to-guy needs for all your conveyancing needs in the south of the island.

In the likely event that you don't have enough money to purchase a property outright, you're going to require a mortgage (*préstamo hipotecario*). Your lawyer will advise you here but as in your home country, it's a good idea to shop around the various lenders. Take your pick from a selection of Canarian (*CajaCanarias*), national (*BBVA*), and international (Barclays) banks. Most offer mortgages with variable interest rates lasting up to 40 years.

In these scrimp-and-save times, the banks aren't willing to lend to any Tomás, Diego or Henrique. Before they hand out the paper as in money, they want to see your paper as in records. So, remember to turn up for your appointment with wage slips from the last three months and bank statements dating back half a year. The test is more stringent if you're self-employed with an auditor's-stamped copy of your last three years of accounts, a year's worth of business bank statements, plus personal bank statements covering the last six months.

What the bank wants to see is that you're able to repay what you borrow. Your liabilities mustn't exceed 35% of your monthly salary. So, if you earn say, €1,000 a month (as around half those employed do) you'll be expected to pay back €350 on a monthly basis. You'll also have to provide the name and contact details of a local guarantor (*aval*).

Many people buy property in the south of the island to rent out as holiday accommodation if they're planning on dividing time between Gran Canaria and their home country. Or they buy a bigger house with the express purpose of converting it into a bed and breakfast. Bear in mind, however, that banks don't count estimated earnings from such ventures as proof of income.

If you're contemplating making the step from tourist to resident, try and travel light. Removal firms do exist on the island but they're best employed if you move from one property to another on Gran Canaria, rather than from abroad. International removal firms such as Pickfords (www.pickfords.com) are a better bet. In general, though, shipping by air freight is quicker but more expensive which suits lighter loads. Meanwhile, dispatching by ship freight's slower but cheaper which rewards those with bulkier possessions.

Council tax doesn't exist in the Canaries. However, if you're in a flat, bear in mind that you'll have to pay *comunidad* which covers the general costs of the whole complex including lighting. In more exclusive areas, expect to pay up to €200 a month. Half that figure for less pricy suburbs.

As regards recycling and general rubbish, bin men don't pick up at individual properties. Mainly this is because in Las Palmas and the major southern resorts at least, most people seem to live in flats. But this is true of rural locations too. Yet every main street has at least one bin for non-recyclable rubbish, a yellow receptacle for plastic, blue for paper, and green for glass. The local council has recently introduced bins which take used olive oil (apparently, you're only recommended to re-use it a maximum of three times). If you can't find any bins or recycling facilities where you are, a trip to the opticians might be in order.

Home Alone – Vega de San Mateo

Helping Hands

Living in Gran Canaria has been a baptism of fire, yet with as many good experiences as bad ones. But be warned, if you come here before securing a job, it will be an uphill struggle. Work is hard to come by and there's a shortage of fixed employment.

As a language teacher it was a little easier for me to settle here, but even then it was very difficult. The contracts are so short that one cannot plan for the future, e.g mortgage payments etc. In addition, I had a dependent child, my son, James, who was then 16 years old and in a Spanish school.

The other aspects to overcome too are primarily the Canarian attitude, customs, legal stipulations and the

47

language barrier. Therefore, misunderstandings will occur. Tourism in Gran Canaria is still a relatively new concept, with the first non-Spanish holidaymakers to its shores arriving little over than 40 years ago. The Canarian people are still getting accustomed to foreigners settling here, and whilst your new neighbours might give you a warm welcome – their bureaucratic counterparts certainly won't. 10 years ago, when we arrived here on the island, there were no facilities offered for us to integrate into the community. One had to find your own way around the constant problems. Ten years on, there is more help offered and a little more understanding towards new settlers, but, there is still room for improvement.

In view of my own experiences in settling into Gran Canaria, I started up an Interactive Social Language Club. We meet every Friday evening from 8pm. The venue is at *Café Los Reyes de Los Pinchitos,* CC Bellavista, San Fernando. The objectives are to help new people of all nationalities to integrate into the local community with as less stress as possible, helping them to produce a quality Curriculum Vitae (which is the most important 'tool' for landing a job to learn interview), interview techniques, understand body language, analyze hidden aspects of a job advert, and so on. All these skills I acquired as a Job Club Leader in London.

At the weekly conversation social sessions we speak Spanish for about 20 minutes and vice versa in English. The topics vary and sometimes conversations get carried away. Friendships are developed, business contacts are made, work information circulated and language skills are improved step by step in a friendly, secure and happy environment.

Hopefully, giving that my settling in here was achieved the hard way, I'll be able to pave an easier way for the newcomers. The secret in contentment here is to help each other to help themselves.

Gilda Larkin-Sealey Contact Gilda on 680 39 10 69/ trainingdevelopment@hotmail.com for further details.

WORKING

Your English will stand you in good stead for a position in the south with regularish service-industy work. It will also come in handy up north. But instead of being called to the bar, so to speak, you'll find plenty of schools eager to employ you. The private bi-lingual (Colegio Arenas, Hispano Ingles) schools will be interested in hiring you for your ability to speak your mother tongue rather than any teaching experience.

I recall an interview I had at one in which the interviewer told me: "We're really impressed with your CV, particularly your work with Spanish teenagers." A summer job, which lasted a mere two days. But be warned, these schools fire as quickly as they hire. A friend of mine, let's call him Martin for that's his name, recalls the weekly staff meeting ending with, "And one last thing on the agenda, don't bother turning up for work tomorrow, Martin."

The private English/American schools (British School, Oakley College) offer a rather more stable employment.

You might also wish to consider teaching in the *colegios publicos* (state schools). But getting a job in one is harder than you think. For a start, even if you hold a teaching qualification, you're going to have to take some incredibly competitive exams known as *oposiciones*. Opponents claim this test more one's knowledge of a subject than aptitude to teach, but you're not going to land a post without passing them. Even then, you're only guaranteed a job close to where you live if you score incredibly highly. Phil, an old work colleague of mine, landed a position in Lanzarote. Suffice to add, but don't even consider applying for *oposiciones* unless you speak anything over 99.9% fluent Spanish.

If you're relocating from a EC country, there's no need to apply for a work permit. But for non-EU residents, it's best to consult your nearest Spanish embassy. European nationals also must register with the Canarian police if they intend to stay longer than three months.

The Spanish social security system includes the usual non-US perks of sick pay, pension, maternity and paternity leave, and unemployment benefit. You'll need a *NIE, Numero de Identidad de Extranjeros*, essentially a certificate which proves you're a foreign national resident in Gran Canaria. Employers will pay your social security contributions if you're on a fixed contract. However, some will pay part of your salary cash in hand in order to get round this.

Initially, employers normally offer rolling contracts of up to three months. They can do this a maximum of four times in a row, as after a year of this, Spanish employment law dictates that you get a fixed contract. Crafty employers though, ordinarily lay off workers for six weeks, in which you're entitled to claim unemployment benefit before employing you on a rolling contract again. The concept of the minimum wage doesn't seem to have hit Canarian shores yet either. I've even been offered as low as €4 a hour for cash-in-hand teaching work – less than half what your average cleaner makes.

A way to avoid such job insecurity is to start your own business. My wife and I run an English-language academy in Las Palmas, Play School (*Calle Senador Castillo Olivares* 48; 928 38 39 91; www.play-school.es). Although we weren't exactly pioneers, others have followed in our footsteps.

Unfortunately, a new start-up is not as easy as ABC. Indeed, you'll be, at the risk of mixing my metaphors, stumped by a forest of paperwork. First, you'll need to apply for a certificate issued by the *Registro Mercantil Central (*Central Commercial Registry). This ensures you're able to confirm the name of your intended business isn't already registered. Step two involves a trip to your local tax office, the misleadingly exotic-sounding *Delegacion de Hacienda*. Here, you'll be able to apply for your *CIF, Certificado de Identificación Fisca,* (company tax identification code).

Next, open a bank account in your company's name. Depending on what your business is, you'll have to deposit a minimum amount, ordinarily €3,000. In order to unglaze your eyes, I'll summarize the remaining steps. These include signing a deed of incorporation in front of a notary, paying transfer tax, registering the company at the Corporate Registry (*Registro Mercantil*) before returning to the *Delegacion de Hacienda* to file a formal declaration of your intention to begin trading.

Further steps include a visit to the Regional Work Authorities Office (*Direccion Provincial de Trabajo*) to communicate the exact date your business opens. To obtain a fuller picture, arrange an appointment with a local lawyer. If anybody knows how to cut red tape, they do.

After setting up your business, you're going to need to promote it. We're lucky as our position opposite and next to two English-language bookshops brings a steady knock on our door. As does our proximity to a number of schools. Nevertheless, my arty wife Cristina designs leaflets and posters to further spread the word. And a website designer Nick Iredale (www.square-sun.net) ensures an Internet presence. Although we haven't, many new businesses submit their details to Yellow Pages, *Paginas Amarillas*, (www.paginasamarillas.es) for even more exposure. Our first class consisted of one boy by himself but we've since grown to having around 100 students.

Even though we're self-employed, we still need to make social security payments. These work out at just over

€200 a month. Another headache is the *Impuesto sobre la Renta de las personas físicas*, more commonly shortened to *Renta*. This is the compulsory annual tax return. You have to submit this between the beginning of March and the end of June. As with many other things, the earlier you do it; the better. This is something you can do yourself, by requesting a *borrador* (draft tax return) from the *Agencia Tributaria* (essentially the tax police). As we own a property and have children, we employ a *gestor* (accountant) so we don't miss out on any much-needed tax breaks.

MONEY

With money too tight to, ahem, mention, banks are as keen for your business as you are for theirs. It's a relatively straightforward procedure to open a bank account. Simply pitch up at the *banco* of your choice with your *Número de Identificación de Extranjero* (*NIE*) number, passport, and proof of address, and you can set up an account there and then.

Non-residents are also able to open an account in Gran Canaria. This might suit frequent travellers to these shores who want to avoid the hassle of changing money. Visit a police station with your passport and photocopy to obtain a non-resident's certificate.

Although slow to pick up on the trend, GC has finally embraced Internet banking. But the traditional way of banking persists. If you have a friend who knows someone who works in a bank, exploit that as it might help you to borrow money with lenders more likely to extend a helping hand to a face they recognize over one they don't.

There's a good selection of banks with branches on Gran Canaria. From the local (*Caja Rural de Canarias*) to national (*Santander*) to international (*Deutsche Bank*), there's also the relatively new Internet-focused *Bankia* which came about after *Caja Madrid* merged with local competitors nationwide including *La Caja de Canarias*. All offer a range of accounts including current and savings, along with credit cards. You can also exchange currency at your branch of choice, along with paying household bills. Most transactions can be done online or at an ATM, but for peace of mind head for a cashier. Make straightforward transfers or withdrawals at the *ventana* (window) while the more complex stuff requires a visit to a *mesa* (table).

GETTING CONNECTED

Gran Canaria is certainly a lot more Internet-savvy than when I first moved here in 2004. In the UK I bought most of what I needed/wanted online. When I arrived, a friend told me she kept a separate bank account for online purchases which she topped up as and when required. Looking back, this makes sense but at the time I couldn't understand why she was so paranoid about shopping online.

The main ISP's *Telefonica* who provide phone lines to most business and residential addresses. *Orange* are another alternative for all your broadband needs. And if you're dongled-up, you can set up a pay-as-you-go 3G connection with providers such as *Vodafone* and *Yoigo*.

Locate free wifi areas in the higher-star hotels and the newer cafes/restaurants. Las Palmas and the major resorts guarantee good mobile reception, but you'll experience lack of coverage in more out-of-the-way zones. My mobile always dies on me when I hit isolated beaches like *Caleta Arriba* and *Güigüi*, for example.

Movistar and *Vodafone* are the biggest mobile networks on the island. Generally, it's cheaper to use *Movistar* and you can buy their sim cards in the plethora of mobile phone shops and newsagents. Using a local sim card means you avoid paying if someone from the UK rings you. If you're using a UK sim card, prepare to be stung.

In Las Palmas and the major resorts you're never far from an Internet cafe. Expect to be charged between €0.50 and €1 for half an hour. There are also terminals in the larger hotels for guests to use.

Workaholics can keep in touch with those of a like mind at the weekly *Interactive Social Language Group* meetings held every Friday at the *Café Los Reyes de Los Pinchitos* in San Fernando. Here from 8 pm onwards, Gilda Larkin-Sealey and friends network over drinks and tapas, discussing, amongst other things, the latest employment opportunities. Contact Gilda on 680 39 10 69/ trainingdevelopment@hotmail.com for further details.

HEALTHCARE

As a tourist, you're entitled to free basic healthcare as received by local residents. As long as you show your EHIC (European Health Insurance Card) and passport. There are many English-speaking doctors. Your hotel will always be able to recommend one. Visitors would be well advised, however, to contact the British Medical Clinic in Puerto Rico (*Avenída Roca Bosch* 4; 928 56 00 16; www. britishmedicalclinic.com). As well as offering private medical services, they provide translations of any tests you may have taken at a Spanish surgery or hospital.

For minor complaints, the local chemists (*farmacias*), recognisable by a green-cross sign, will stock just about anything you may require and there's always one open after hours in each area. The location of the duty chemist's clearly indicated on every chemist's door.

One of our major concerns about relocating from the UK was the level of care our then youngest son Alex would receive. He'd been diagnosed with leukaemia aged just eight months and had spent half a year in Great Ormond Street Hospital. At GOSH, he'd been looked after by one of the world's leading authorities on childhood leukaemia. But we were assured the hospital in Gran Canaria Alex would be regularly attending followed exactly the same programme of treatment as Great Ormond Street.

In our first year here, I escorted Alex to the *Hospital Universitario Materno Infantil* (*Avenida Marítima del Sur*

S/N; 928 44 45 00), *Materno* for short, on a weekly basis. Although my wife and I have attended more funerals here than either of us would like to, it's clearly the disease that's to blame. The establishment's standard of medical care's second to none.

Residents should register with their nearest *centro de salud* (health centre). They'll refer those with more serious conditions to a hospital. There are two main hospitals in Las Palmas. You'll find the older *Complejo Hospitalario Universitario Insular* (928 44 40 00) on the Avenida Marítima del Sur, just as you leave Las Palmas heading in the direction of the airport and the south. Closer to *Canteras* beach and the motorway to Agaete is where you'll discover the newer *Complejo Hospitalario Doctor Negrin* (*Plaza Barranco la Ballena S/N*; 928 45 00 00). In the south, the *Hospital San Roque Maspalomas* (*Calle Mar de Siberia* 1, 928 06 36 00) in Meloneras caters for both private and public patients.

Staff do their best to offer an English-speaking option. My wife, to her despair, once served as a translator at the *Materno* when a girl from the UK had a fatal accident in a resort swimming pool. To be on the safe side, it's best to visit the health centres or hospitals with a native Spanish speaker.

Out of our three children, two were born here on the island. Both in the *Hospital Insular*. While some of my wife's well-to-do friends favour the *Clinica Santa Catalina* (*Calle León y Castillo* 292; 928 24 51 26), Cristina pours scorn on the extra cost incurred especially as if there any complications, you're immediately transferred to the public hospital.

Dental care's rather more problematic. The *dentistas* in Gran Canaria are private, so it might well be worth investing in some dental-health insurance. Otherwise, when you need some work done; you'll avoid the risk of an accompanying heart attack.

Now play your way out of those bunkers

STAYING THERE FOREVER (RETIRING)

It's not quite a Spanish Florida (that would be Tenerife) but Gran Canaria is becoming an ever-more popular retirement destination. For every pro (the sun), though, there's a con (isolation). When we lived in the UK, for example, the weekend (football permitting) was an excuse for a cheapo, long weekend in mainland Europe. Because of the Canaries' location, this isn't an affordable option.

Consider that while your loved ones will be still be able to reach you by phone, by car is now out of the question. Flights from northern European countries average around four hours. Although in and around the southern resorts, there are expat communities aging from gap-year travellers up to senior citizens to make you feel more at home than you might have imagined.

For those of advanced years, there are a good selection of *residencias de personas majores* (residential homes) especially if you're living in the north of the island. Possibly my favourite street in Las Palmas, *Calle Perojo*, boasts *Ballesol* (928 38 44 66; www.ballesol.es), one of the group's many *centros residenciales para la 3a edad*. When they were first converting this, I was curious of what it was to become: bar, nightclub, restaurant? Residential home I hadn't bargained on.

You're entitled to the state pension you set up in your country of origin should you decide to relocate to Gran Canaria. Open a Spanish bank account to receive your pension in *euros*. If you relocate to Gran Canaria before pensionable age, you can pay into your existing pension plan and/or into a Spanish one.

If you're retired, you qualify for a free *tarjeta mensual de jubilado* which allows you to make 100 journeys a month on the distinctive yellow Las Palmas buses, *Guaguas Municipales*. Elsewhere on the island, if you're aged 70 or over, you can enjoy discounted travel on the blue *Global* buses. These *guaguas* connect the south with the north, and everywhere else in-between.

A mecca for arthritis and MS sufferers, Gran Canaria's warmer climes offer immense therapeutic value. Apply for an EHIC (European Health Insurance Card) to cover your basic healthcare needs.

EDUCATION

Relocating with school-age children is more difficult than without them. They'll be leaving friends behind, many of them they've been inseparable from since birth. Although your kids won't have any trouble finding penpals.

Having worked in both the public and private educational sectors in Gran Canaria, I'm a fan of the *colegios publicos* (state schools) where pupils come from a variety of backgrounds, both racial and socio-economic. But you should sign up your children for Spanish lessons well before your move to familiarize their ears and mouths with what they're going to be hearing/talking. Because, with the exception of English, French, and German classes, teachers give lessons in the island's native tongue.

If you want your children to receive exactly the same education as they would in your home country, be prepared to pay the price of *colegios privados* (private schools). There are English schools in Gran Canaria which follow the UK National Curriculum. The largest of these is the Canterbury School (*Lugar Lomo el Diviso S/N*; 928 43 98 10; www.canterbury-school.com) with an infants in Las Palmas, a primary and secondary in San Lorenzo, and a primary in Maspalomas. In Tafira Baja, you'll find the slightly older British School of Gran Canaria (*Carretera Marzagan S/N*; 928 35 11 67; www.bs-gc.net). While in Tafira Alta, Donat Morgan (who impressed me the most/ gave the best soundbites when I was commissioned to write an article about private education for *RTN Canarias*) runs Oakley College (*Calle Zuloaga* 17; 928 35 42 47; www.oakleycollege.com).

US expats can enrol their children at The American School of Las Palmas *(Carretera de los Hoyos KM 1.7*; 928 43 00 23; www.aslp.org) which runs a fantastic Food Fair in the summer offering a taste of the establishment – in more ways than one. Almatriche, meanwhile, houses the island's only official German school, *Deutsche Schule Las Palmas* (*Lomo del Drago S/N*; 928 67 07 50; www.dslpa.org) providing a bilingual education from infants upwards. It's worth bearing in mind that all these schools, along with the bilingual *Colegio Arenas* (www.colegioarenas.es), supply free education to their teachers' children.

The *guarderias infantiles* (nurseries) accept children from 0 to 6 years old. Many now are bilingual (English/Spanish) with most including an introduction to English at the very least. Both our older children went to *Pizquito* (*Calle Cano 9*, Las Palmas; 928 38 15 91) located in a pretty pedestrianized street off the main shopping area of Triana. Gustavo kindly found a place for Dani who travelled in advance of us, staying with his aunt while we cared for Alex during his spell in Great Ormond Steet.

As well as elementary education, nurseries are as much about childcare. Take *Pizquito* which opens from seven o'clock in the morning to half past six in the evening. The nurseries also care for older children as the *colegio publicos* finish earlier than their private counterparts – for example, La Manzana (*Calle de Obispo Rabadan* 48; 928 37 17 24; www.la-manzana.com) arranges pick-ups at the major schools in the Arenales area of Las Palmas.

Children typically start at school in the year they turn three. My nephew Guillermo still aged two began at *Colegio Teresiano* (Calle Pio XII 34, Las Palmas; 928 29 30 14; teresianolaspalmas.teresianas.info) as he was going to be three in December of that year. This *colegio concertado* (state-assisted school) contains the majority of his cousins, my two eldest sons included. Beginning in the infants, he'll pass through to the primary department, and then secondary school – all of which are housed within the same building.

If your kids attend a *colegio publico*, things are a little bit different. True, they'll begin their education in the year they turn three. But they'll leave in the year they turn 12, transferring to an *instituto de educacion secundaria*. Here, they're given a lot more freedom/responsibility than a *CP* which is a turn-off for as many parents as it's a turn-on for others.

There's just the one university on the island at which children may complete their tertiary education, the *Universidad de Las Palmas de Gran Canaria* (*Calle Juan de Quesada* 30; 928 45 10 00; www.ulpgc.es). Unlike in your home country, this is largely made up of Canarian natives, which has as much to do with the Spanish child not leaving their familial home until they get married as anything else. This university also welcomes mature students, with my mother-in-law a member of its recent alumni.

If you're a parent of a child with special needs it's essential you translate any documents you have from your previous educational authority into Spanish for the purpose of informing your child's new school. Spanish educational laws stipulate that special needs and disabled students should be fully integrated into mainstream schools wherever possible. When I worked at *CP Bañaderos*, there was a lovely girl whose carer used to attend the English lessons with her. In other schools I've worked at some of the children are pulled out of English for specialist sessions with the *apoyo* (support teacher). There's probably more segregation in private schools with special needs children being educated in separate classrooms.

For the most extreme cases, Las Palmas and Telde house a number of special schools. Worth your while contacting are the *Fundacion Canaria el Patio* (Calle Murga 8, 1D, Las Palmas; 928 36 80 01; www.procesoelpatio.org) and *Centro Específico Petra Lorenzo* (Calle Cruz de Jerez SN, Telde; 928 68 54 40). These establishments cater for statemented children.

As well as adult-education classes in subjects as diverse as art, cooking and languages, there are a number of *colegios profesionales*. Perfect for those contemplating a change in career, you're able to retrain as a dentist, engineer, or lawyer. Amongst many other professions which also include chemists, estate agents, and vets. A girl who worked on the classroom assistants' project with me left to study to become a nurse. Others, noting the discrepancy in pay, took their *oposiciones* (exams held to fill vacancies in the public sector) to become teachers.

The Beautiful Game

On a Wednesday night at 10 0'clock, the last thing you feel like doing is playing a game of football. In the Gran Canarian Veteran's League this is perfectly normal. This may seem bad enough, but then consider sitting on the bench for the whole of the first half. You eventually get your first kick at 11 pm. During the first few weeks of my two seasons as the only *guiri* (foreigner) in an 11-a-side team this would happen a lot. *"Gorrdon, la Segunda,"* became a familiar instruction from the captain.

This was Juani, a larger-than-life character who didn't exactly stand on ceremony. After one game in which I failed to tackle an opponent, allowing him to score a winning goal in the last minute, he shouted, from the other side of the pitch, *"Gorrdon, voy a matarte!"*

After a few more steps towards the changing room I realised he had just told me he was going to kill me and wondered whether it may be worth bypassing the post-match drink. Fortunately he didn't and all was forgotten by the next match where, as usual he greeted me with a big grin and an exclamation of *"El Inglés!"*

As centre-back, Juani clearly expected the rest of the defence to follow his no-nonsense style of play, but further up the pitch there were some extremely skilful players. Bolo, for example, pony-tailed, unshaven with his shirt tucked outside his shorts played in midfield with style and grace that belied his appearance, and scored some spectacular long-range goals. Sometimes I could give him a short pass to him on the halfway line and would end up being able to count it as an assist as I analysed the game in my head on the way home.

As well as the late kick-offs, I had to get used to playing on astroturf on a regular basis as grass is at a premium in Gran Canaria. Seemingly expensive, unused golf courses are the only facility for which it is deemed necessary. There were also some games played on a kind of treacherous gravel on which staying upright was a task in itself.

Generally though, the facilities, such as the changing rooms were far superior to England and pitches were often set against a scenic mountainous backdrop. Consequently I rarely pined for the playing fields of South London. Besides, it was never a good idea to sit on a bench in Clapham Common until 11 pm.

Gordon Sutcliffe, Read more Gordon at www.thecanarynews.com

Life's a beach

LEISURE ACTIVITIES

You'll have just as much excuse to get fit, what with the excellent leisure facilities, on the island as to get fat, what with the sometimes stodgy food and *siesta*-inducing sunshine. There' a *polideportivo* (sports centre) in most municipalities but Canarians like to keep trim even while on the beach. Look out for the beach walkers who walk from one end of the *playa* to the other. On repeat.

The *polideportivos* I know best are in Las Palmas and Santa Brigida. Both have excellent spa facilities. The *Complejo Deportivo Las Rehoyas* (*Carretera Antigua del Norte S/N,* Las Palmas; 928 36 22 38; www.complejolasrehoyas.com) also features one of the only football pitches remaining open to the public when there's not a match on.

As well as there being many private clubs, you can play *padel* at most *polideportivos/complejos deportivos* (sport complexes). It's a way of bringing this posh sport, a mix of squash and tennis, to the masses I suppose. And considering the cost of the equipment you'll need to buy to play, hiring's a much more attractive option.

Your children can learn to paddle and beyond in one of the island's many swimming clubs. Ours used to go, during their summer holidays. But as they're held in swimming pools, we tired of the inevitable ear infections they used to pick up and plan to teach new recruit Tom in the open sea instead.

The Canarians are very much the Antipodeans of the Northern Hemisphere. So if you want to fit in, you're going to have to try surfing. Both my two elder children and I learned to do so at Oceanside (*Calle Almansa 14*, Las Palmas; 928 22 04 37; www.grancanariasurf.es). Teaching you safety and basic technique, you can also hone your surf skills by buying or hiring a board from their shop.

Choose a membership package at a wide selection of gyms. You'd probably expect more chains on Gran Canaria, but they're conspicuous by their absence. A good independent *gimnasio* for those in the south at least is *Beach Gym* (*Centro Comercial San Agustín;* 928 76 29 41; www.beachgym.es), catering for all your workout needs.

Most parents enrol their boys in football teams. Having played in a number of different clubs, our eldest two boys have found a happy home at *CD Vegueta Arbol Bonito* (*Calle Cordoba* 31A, Las Palmas; 928 33 40 48; www.cd-vegueta-arbol-bonito.com.es). Their father, meanwhile, plays in the veteran's league but don't expect any contact details as further competition for places is the last thing I need.

Ballet remains a popular recreation for girls, although there're increasing numbers of *Billy Elliot* wannabes. Sign up for your child to learn more modern dance forms at *La Escuela de Danza Moderna* (*Calle Doña Pura Bascarán* 3, Las Palmas; 669 35 67 62; www.escueladanzanayraruiz.com). A more neutral choice's enrolling your child at a *club de artes marciales* (martial arts club) which may be useful in keeping the local bullies at bay.

"Gran Canaria lives up to its nickname of a miniature continent. The island is very green and agricultural in the north, the centre has forests, lakes and several villages of inhabited cave houses. The south has some spectacular scenery across uninhabited ravines and canyons, known as Barrancos, and there are several large volcanic craters, known as Calderas. Many of the footpaths you will be walking on are old donkey tracks, known as Camino Reales. There used to be a large network of tracks connecting all the villages and towns together, often by much shorter and direct routes than the modern roads that have replaced them.

The beauty of the real Gran Canaria is in the heart of the island and is unimaginable from the motorway that connects the airport to large resorts of hotels and apartments, bars and restaurants etc. in the barren south and east of the island." Rambling Roger (Bradley) advises you to walk this way.

FIESTA CALENDAR

Día de los Reyes (King's Day) Whole Island 6th January

Carnaval de Las Palmas (Las Palmas Carnival) Las Palmas Dates vary each year

Fiestas de Almendro en Flor (Blossoming Almond Festival) Valsequillo February

Carnaval de Maspalomas (Maspalomas Carnival) Maspalomas Dates very each year

Día de San José (St Joseph's/Father's Day) Whole Island 19th March

Fiesta de los Aborgines Whole Island 29th April

Fiestas del Queso (Cheese Festival) Santa María de Guía April-May

Día de Canarias (Canarian Day) Whole Island 30th May

Corpus Christi Whole Island May-June

Fiesta del Carmen Whole Island August

Bajada de la Rama (Bringing Down The Branches) Agaete August

Fiesta de la Nuestra Señora del Pino (Our Lady of the Pine Festival) Teror 8th September

Fiesta del Charco (Festival of the Lagoon) Puerto de la Aldea 11th September

Fiestas de la Navel (Naval Festival) Las Palmas and the other ports on the island 2nd Saturday of October

Día de Santa Lucía (St Lucy's Day) Santa Lucía de Tirajana 13th December

Seasons in the Sun

After more than 20 years residing on Gran Canaria, I can honestly say there are few things British which I miss with any notable emotion apart from the changing of the seasons and, if I have to admit it, fish and chips. It's the same every year as the months tick by, the pages get torn off the stub and the calender gets thinner.

April and memories of green shoots, trees budding and daffodils sometimes cause a momentary bout of homesickness. Sigh. A pang for green fields stabs hard, but soon passes. September and October heading into November brings with them the longing for a proper autumn. Foggy breath on the window-screen and frost-bitten fingertips might not seem something you'd ever miss, but after 22 years of blistering heat, well...

Put it down to my poetic heart, but living in Gran Canaria's constant and unchanging climate, leaves me without a lot of inspiration for filling the stanzas. Blue skies, the sway of palm trees and constant sunshine are beautiful, but limiting when it comes to scribing verse.

From sheer necessity, I've developed my own method of denoting the changing of the seasons. They don't always coincide exactly with the meteorological ones, but never mind. For lack of visual alterations in the surrounding landscape, I now mark the passing of the seasons using the customers I serve on a daily basis as a barometer. Café Central, the restaurant where I work, is a busy place and the daily comings and goings are frequent enough to make sure I get, more or less, an accurate reading. Winter, like a British Christmas, has become associated with its own unique and wonderful aromas. To be honest, it's mostly those of warm whisky and ground cinnamon floating up from the glasses of Irish Coffees on my tray.

Spring's on its way when, similar to waking up from a long hibernation, the customers slowly start to speak a language I can understand and the tangy scent of fresh mint crushed with lemon assails my delicate nostrils. Luckily, it's still cool enough not to melt the ice in the glasses before I can get the *mojitos* on the table. Summer is easily identified. The whimpers of the customers when they sit down and their sunburn stings, plus an accompanying waft of aftersun lotion, is a dead give-away. Just in case I'm mistaken, I usually wait for the vocal confirmation which goes something like, "Have you got John Smith's on draught, mate?"

LizX, Inside Expert, <u>www.grancanaria.co.uk</u> and author of The Dove, The Dragon and The Flame, <u>www.authonomy.com/books/36518/the-dove-the-dragon-and-the-flame</u>

MAKING YOURSELF AT HOME PLANS

Families

Weekend

Invest in a two-parks ticket and spend a Saturday enjoying the shows featuring dolphins, parrots, birds of prey and exotic birds at shady *Palmitos Park* (*Barranco de Los Palmitos S/N*; 928 797 070; www.palmitospark.es) in Maspalomas. Reapply sun cream liberally at *Aqualand Maspalomas* (*Carretera Palmitos Park KM 3*; 928 14 05 25; www.aqualand.es) on Sunday, not forgetting to take your flip flops with you unless you want scorched soles as a souvenir, and cool off your hot bod on the panopoly of rides and slides.

Week

You're in for a bumpy ride at *Camello Fataga* (*Carretera Palmitos Park 6*; 928 76 07 81; www.camellosafari.com). This Camel Safari is certainly family-friendly though. We've all heard of car and sea sickness but camel sickness just doesn't exist. The Puerto-Rico-moored *Spirit of the Sea* (928 56 22 29; www.dolphin-whale.com) will satisfy your family's whale watcher. This glass-bottomed boat allows you to enjoy the views of deep-sea divers without getting wet.

Race to the chequered flag at Tarajalillo's *Gran Karting Club* (*Carretera General del Sur* 46; 928 15 71 90;

www.grankarting.com). The 990-metre adult track allows you to reach speeds of up to 80kph, the 650m junior track caters for 12 to 16 year-olds, whilst there's also a children's track with mini-karts for kids aged five and over.

Month

Travel back in time to a pre-Spanish Gran Canaria at *Mundo Aborigen* (*Macizo de Amurga*; 928 17 22 95; www.mundoaborigen.com) in the south of the island. From the great outdoors (with this park being set in the surprisingly verdant mountainous area of Fataga), to the great indoors at Gáldar's *Museo y Parque Arquelógico Cueva Pintada* (*Calle Audiencia* 2; 928 89 57 46; www.cuevapintada.com) which offers a window, quite literally as you'll discover, into the life of the originial inhabitants of the island, the *canarii*. Elsewhere in the north of Gran Canaria, the *Cenobio de Valerón* (*Cuesta de Silva S/N*; 618 60 78 96; www.cenobiodevaleron.com) in Guía provides a further introduction to the island's noble ancestors. This granary's the perfect stop-off on a coastal excursion.

It's not all sun, sun, sun in Gran Canaria (especially so in Las Palmas) but you can still have fun, fun, fun when the weather becomes less hospitable than a wet Wednesday in Whitby. So when it threatens to rain on your parade, head to *Parque Santa Catalina's Museo Elder* (*Parque Santa Catalina S/N*; 828 01 18 28; www.museoelder.org) in the capital. This lilliputian version of London's Science Museum entertains as much as it educates.

For Life

Pantomine doesn't exist on Gran Canaria. Yet they replicate the sweet-throwing escapades during the *Cabalgata de Reyes Magos* (Three Wise Men Parade). Taking place on the 5th of January (the Spanish equivalent of Christmas Eve), catch the best and biggest processions in either Las Palmas or San Fernando de Maspalomas. Neither is there Bonfire Night. But those nostalgic for firewalk displays will enjoy the *Entierro de la Sardina* (Burial of the Sardine) which marks the end of *Carnaval*. Here, following a mock-sombre funeral march of grieving widows (typically men in drag), locals cremate a wooden sardine on a boat off the coast of Las Canteras. A lively flourish of pyrotechnic explosions rounds off the show.

Culture Vultures

Weekend

Boasting the most pedestrian-friendly centre in the whole of Gran Canaria, the beautifully-preserved heart of Arucas is the perfect place for a *paseo* – the stroll beloved of Canarians and arguably the finest Spanish import. Take in the Gaudiesque church, *Iglesia de San Juan Bautista* – an excellent example of its classic architecture. Work up an appetite by continuing your saunter up to the town of Arucas' mountain where you'll be greeted by the Michelin-listed *Meson de la Montaña* (*Montaña de Arucas S/N*; 928 60 08 44; www.mesonarucas.es).

Dress to impress for a cultural night out at Las Palmas' *Auditorio Alfredo Kraus* (*Playa de Las Canteras S/N*; 928 49 11 70; www.auditorio-alfredokraus.com) – taking in an opera, classical musical concert, or jazz gig. Constructed in 1997 by Catalan architect Oscar Tusquets, even Prince Charles, modern architecture's biggest critic, would succumb to its charms. Resembling a giant lighthouse, it acts as a beacon – lighting up the rest of the *Las Canteras* shoreline.

Head to the centre of the island and to Teror which is another town which favours the walk rather than the drive through. The 18th-century *Basilica de Nuestra Señora del Pino*, dedicated to Gran Canaria's patron saint, is as impressive inside as outside. The beautifully-restored *Plaza Teresa de Bolivar* doubles as a marketplace on Sunday.

Week
Marvel at the sculpture promenade which extends from Agüimes's *casco histórico*, historic quarter, to its coast. These include AL Benítez's donkey and lovers (two separate sculptures) and W Herrera García's camel. Although these are modern sculptures, they blend perfectly into a background dating back to 1486.

See the beautiful swan develop from Las Palmas's ugly duckling with a visit to the neighbouring Vegueta and Triana districts, a UNESCO World Heritage Site, stopping at one of the many terraced bars/cafes for a restorative *cortado* (milky espresso) or bite to eat.

Okay, it may be a theme park, but the recreated village to be found at the *Pueblo Canario*, neighbouring the four-star *Hotel Santa Catalina*, hosts performance of traditional Canarian folk music accompanied by morris-style dancing.

Month

There's a long tradition of cave-dwelling in Gran Canaria. Started by the *canarii*, it continues to the present day with the existence of modern-day Flintsones. Have a yabba dabba doo time at the *Centro de Interpretación Arquelógico* (*Barranco de Guayadeque S/N*; 928 17 20 26), an Agüimes museum showcasing the greatest and latest archaeological finds in the area.

The bones and skulls on view at the *Museo Canario* (*Calle Doctor Verneau 2*; 928 33 68 00; www.elmuseocanario.com) in Las Palmas should carry a PG warning. Ditto the mummies. Open to 8pm Monday to Friday, it's best not to visit during a full moon.

They've been quaffing wine on Gran Canaria since the Spanish invasion. Indeed overindulging in the local tipple appears to be a practice that has been going on for years, even as far back as Shakespearean times. The Bard indelicately describes *Falstaff* in *The Merry Wives of Windsor*, for example, as *"given over to fornication, taverns, Canarian wine and the wind"*. Whilst it's no Loire Valley, the Gran Canaria Wine Route (www.grancanaria. com/patronato_turismo/The-Wine-Route.2532.0.html), particularly the Bandama, Santa Brigada and San Mateo sections, is well worth taking.

For Life

Drop by Las Palmas' *Casa África* (*Calle Alfonso XIII 5*; 928 43 28 00; www.casafrica.es), motto *África y España, cada vez más cerca* (Africa and Spain, getting closer every day), an emblematic building which houses regular exhibitions of African art, film and photography.

August's *Cine+Food* (www.cinemasfood.com) allows you to watch films on big screens accompanied by more than the usual choice of hot dogs, nachos, and popcorn. *Parque Santa Catalina* in Las Palmas houses stalls from an eclectic selection of local restaurants. The cinema aspect of the equation is free but you have to pay for your food.

You'd be a fool not to visit the folly that is *Castillo de la Fortaleza* (*Calle Tomás Arroyo Cardoso S/N*; 928 79 83 10) in *Santa Lucía de Tirajana*. The brainchild of local, in alphabetical order, archaelogist, artist, collector, and writer, the great, late Vincente Sanchez Araña, it's a bonsai version of a medieval castle. Constructed in the mid-20th century, the 16 rooms comprising Araña's erstwhile home include an artillery, art gallery, and botany collection.

Rooms with a view – Vega de San Mateo

Nature Lovers

Weekend

Follow in the footsteps of 16th-century Flemish merchant Daniel Van Damme by descending 200 metres to the bottom of the *Caldera de Bandama*. This crater's named after Van Damme who first planted vines there. A half-hour trek will reward you with sights of volcanic ash, endemic botanic species and even an abandoned farm.

Fawn over the flora on display at Tafira's *Jardín Botánico Viera y Clavijo* (*Carretera del Centro KM 7*; 928 21 95 80; www.jardincanario.org). The current director of this botanic garden, Dr David Bramwell MBE, in a past life was a bouncer at Liverpool's famous Cavern Club. A living monument to native Canarian vegetation, Bramwell and his team devote their time to the conservation, growing and studying of the 2,000 species of plants, 500 of which are unique to the island.

Off the road that links Arucas to its nearest beach, El Puertillo, you'll come across the *Jardín de la Marquesa* (*Lugar Hoyas 2*; 928 60 44 86; www.jardindelamarquesa.com), the Marchioness' Garden. Belonging to the palatial *Casa de la Marquesa* which dates back to 1880, these Romantic-style gardens are open to the public from Monday to Saturday 9 am to 1 pm and from 2 to 6 pm – but it's best to book in advance online. Guided tours can be arranged for groups numbering over 30 and the beautiful setting's unsurprisingly a popular choice for wedding receptions.

Week

Not for nothing is Gran Canaria known as a mini continent. And the isolated westerly beach of *Güigüi*'s a world away from the package-tour hell more commonly associated with the island. For die-hard trekkers, it's best to head off from La Aldea de San Nicolás' *El Tarahalillo*. Follow the well-signposted route to *Go-Guy* and depending how much you're carrying (we're talking weight as well as baggage), you'll arrive at *Güigüi Grande* between four and six hours later. This is not your final destination however as the more picturesque *Güigüi Chico* lies just around the corner.

Contact the *Finca de Osorio* (928 63 00 90), a couple of kilometres from the centre of Teror, in advance to reserve a picnic space. Walk off your *alfresco* lunch by exploring the 207 hectares, made up of paths, mountains, ravines, and forest. Those with a head for heights are advised to take the turning to the *Pico (Peak) de Osorio* where having ascended 968 metres you'll be invited to further make your mark by signing a guestbook.

Another popular place to eat out(side) is *La Laguna de Valleseco*. Get in touch with the *Ayuntamiento de Valleseco* (928 61 80 22) before visiting to use their barbecue facilities. Work off your barbie with a mountain-bike ride, with the surrounding *Parque Rural de Doramas* providing the perfect terrain.

Month

The loftiest village on the island, Artenara, provides plenty of highs. And they're all natural. Use it as a base to explore the surprisingly verdant *Montaña del Brezo*, the emblematic needle-thin *Roque Bentayga* where the natives made their last stand against the Spanish invasion force, and the *Barranco de la Mina*, a truly grand canyon.

Explore the ravines which connect Arteara and Ayagaures, the *barrancos de Los Vicentes and Los Decentillos*. This 10km-hike follows a gently undulating path through one of Gran Canaria's most forested areas. With a drop of a mere 50 metres, even vertigo sufferers can enjoy this trek.

Go green by visiting the verdant *Llanos de Juan Martín* of *Las Mesillas*. Surveying the sheep roaming this area, you could be forgiven for thinking you were in the Brecon Beacons. Until you look up and see the sun in the sky.

For Life

The ironically-named *Valleseco* (Dry Valley) is anything but. Wellies are required to truly appreciate the wet and wonderful *Barranco de Azuaje*. The *charcos* (pools) here are not only topped up by streams but by the fact this area has the highest rainfall on the whole island.

Not to be confused with the rather more prosaic district of the same name in Las Palmas, *Altavista* in the centre of Gran Canaria offers an even higher view. When you finally ascend, you'll be treated to a panorama taking in the postcard-famous *Roque Nublo*, the Acusa plain and La Aldea de San Nicolás, the island's main agricultural region.

There aren't any lakes in Gran Canaria. But the man-made variety, the *presas* (reservoirs) will fool you into thinking otherwise, especially as they're set in areas of outstanding natural beauty. Three to see: *Presas de Chira*, *Las Niñas*, and *Soria.*

Mountain High, Valley Low – La Aldea

Surf's Up

"Matthew, come here," instructs Itmar, my surfing coach. "Not that way, *this* way," he beckons while sporting a seen-it-all-before grin. We'd been less than five feet apart from each other. It now appears to be more than 50.

It's Day 2 of my beginners' course at Las Palmas' Ocean Side Surf School. Enrolling seemed a way of further acclimatizing to life over here as Canarians are very much the Australians of the Northern Hemisphere.

"It's an addiction, Matthew," Sergio Alvarez, the school's owner, warns me. "I have to go surfing at least once every day."

Day 1 and I pitch up nice and early. Suited but unbooted, our class heads down to the beach. We begin with a series of warm-up exercises which I'd swear Itmar has lifted from the *Kama Sutra*.

Next comes a drill every surfer needs to learn off by heart: how to board, erm… the board. Itmar demonstrates what we must do. First, he stands to one side of the surfboard, before dropping onto it in one smooth motion. Positioned like he's about to do a press-up, he proceeds to paddle before springing up to stand on the board. Legs akimbo, he thrusts his posterior upwards and then encourages us to do the same. "Come on, I want to see your chicken asses," he demands.

The rest of my first lesson is taken up with trying (and failing) to get on the board, let alone stand up. Head honcho Sergio suggests that by my second or third lesson I'll be standing up. As it turns out, it's day three before I manage to do so. Day 4 and Itmar explains that he's not going to come into the water today. He launches into some spiritual surfer spiel about it being a solo sport, and your only companion being the wave.

While I'm sure he believes all this, I think the temperature of the water has more to do with his decision to stay on the beach.

"It's so cold," he moans. "It's not cold, Itmar," I point out.

"Matthew, you're English," he replies. I'm not sure if the absence of Itmar contributes to my abysmal showing, but I regress to my ineptitude of Day 1.

Day 5 and I'm determined to stand up again and for longer. Yet, when I enter the water, I'm struggling to even get on my board and when I manage to do so, I have to readjust as I'm hitting the board too low, with my feet dangling too much into the water. Itmar calls me back to the shore.

"In one take, Matthew, one take," he reiterates, before showing me how to board for the umpteenth time. His advice pays immediate dividends and I'm standing.

Itmar starts yelling, "Chicken ass, chicken ass!" and I stick out my bottom accordingly. I even smile. Far too early, as I soon topple over into the foam. Clearly, I've still got a lot to learn...

Matthew Hirtes, author *Going Local in Gran Canaria*

Reach for the Sky: Gran Canaria's very own Alps

Sport Enthusiasts

Weekend

You really wouldn't want to be in the spectacularly ugly *Pozo Izquierdo* were it not for the fact it's the major windsurfing centre on the island. After slaloming the waves, the appropriately-named *El Viento* (The Wind) offers a surprisingly varied menu to top up your energy levels. The restaurant's terrace also provides the perfect vantage point for you to show off to your fans/family.

Ease yourself into the underwater world by taking a diving course at one of the schools based near Las Palmas' *Playa de Canteras*. This beach's fine-sand reef provides an excellent barrier against the open sea. So it's less deep-sea diving and more giant-bath diving.

Week

The sky's the limit if you join the paragliders who descend from the hilly suburb of Los Giles, overlooking Las Palmas' stunning *Auditorio Alfredo Kraus*. Come back down to earth without a bump at the *Plaza de la Musica's* stylish *Marea Baja*.

The leisure facilities Las Palmas has to offer are second to none. Head to *Complejo Deportivo Las Rehoyas* (*Carretera Antigua del Norte S/N*; 928 36 22 38; www.complejolasrehoyas.com) to attain that body beautiful. A surface area of 141,560 square metres boasts football pitches, basketball courts, a skate park and so much more.

Month

The surf's always up in Europe's answer to Hawaii. Located at the foot of the famous sand dunes in Maspalomas, the *Surf Canaries Surf School* (*Avenida Alf Provisionales, Anexo II*; 686 21 19 96; www.surf-canaries.com) offers classes for beginners upwards. Ride those waves, baby.

For Life

Despite 'enjoying' the lowest budget of the whole *Liga ACB*, local (Las Palmas) heroes Gran Canaria 2014 consistently overperform. And unlike at the city's football stadium with its atmosphere-draining athletics track, the sound of the fans doesn't disappear into thin air at its 4,500-capacity *Centro Insular de Deportes* (*Avenida José Alcalde Ramírez Bethencourt S/N*; 928 21 95 60; www.cbgrancanaria.net) base. The fact they're almost exclusively home supporters, due to the island's non-proximity to the peninsula, also makes it a more daunting venue for opposing teams.

"*Inglés,* I want to kiss you." Football team-mate José Antonio reacts positively to a goal-line clearance.

Hopeless Romantics

Weekend

Pamper yourselves doolally at the Spa Corallium in the four-star Lopesan Costa Meloneras Resort (*Mar Mediterraneo* 1; 928 12 81 00; www.lopesan.com). The spa's circuit starts at the *Womb Room* aka *Zodiac Relax Room* which is a more sensual experience than you'd imagine. Before taking you on a global tour, featuring an *African Sauna*, *Hamam* (Turkish Bath), *Ice World* and *Igloo*, replete with snow showers, and *Himalayan Salt Cave*.

Playa Amadores may well translate as Lovers' Beach but the less romantically-sounding Patalavaca (Cow's Leg) is actually a better bet to wow your partner. Dress to impress at *Restaurante La Aquarela* (*Barranco de la Verga* 5; 928 73 58 91; www.restaurantelaaquarela.com), smarter than its tucked-away location in the Aquamarina apartment/ bungalow complex suggests. The classicist's four-course gourmet menu will set you back €45 whilst the à la carte menu sees traditional ingredients and modern cooking methods collide to propel you to Gastro Heaven.

Party Animals

Weekend

To generalize, the clubs in the south are a mecca for the tourists staying there whilst the northern clubbing scene attracts the locals. Yet there are Canarians who live in the south and expats like myself based in the north. So it's not as clear-cut as all that.

The two main clubbing areas in the south are the Yumbo (*Avenída de EEUU 54*; 928 76 41 96; www.cc-yumbo. com) and the Kasbah (*Calle de Málaga S/N*; 928 77 63 99). By day, the Yumbo is a run-of-the-mill shopping centre catering for the needs of families holidaying nearby; by night, it's transformed into a Sodom and Gomorrah of writhing gay men, wriggling their bits to the hits in a panoply of bars. By day, the Kasbah looks like a mini-Coventry; by night, it's much the same.

For Life

Channel pantomime, specifically *Cinderella* when it comes to dressing for Las Palmas' winter *Carnaval*. Cinders' *Ugly Stepsisters* are unlikely style icons for partygoers. Join in the cross-dressing at *Parque Santa Catalina* with the biggest parties held at the weekend.

In a rare display of unity, every July the major Canarian islands of Fuerteventura, Gran Canaria, Lanzarote, and Tenerife plus La Palma put on the *Canarias Jazz & Mas* (www.canariasjazz.com). Mas means more and the programme will typically include African bands, DJs and rock groups, as well as jazz in all its forms. Many of the shows are free.

Valley Girl

I sit (coffee in hand) looking out over my balcony across the now green, vertical mountains in 'my' little valley in the centre of Gran Canaria, *Cercado de Espino*. In the *finca* (small farm) across the way, the goats and their kids have been let out to graze and are bounding gleefully up and down the craggy rocks and over the cacti. The cows' tails flash in the bright sunlight as they rhythmically swat away the persistent flies whilst their owners contentedly chew on indigestible banana trees and bamboo shoots thrown to them each morning by the old grumbling pick-up that grinds its way up the vertical concrete track.

I'm looking down over the tree tops, not just any trees though, orchards full of orange, lemon, lime, mango and avocado trees, with their thick, tough, dark-green leaves reflecting the hot sunshine and sheltering the doves, pigeons, parakeets and the little common canary birds, all twittering noisily as they go about their business.

It's February now, but this is the equivalent of our summer back home, when vegetables are growing abundantly around the Spanish village in neat little furrows usually in the most absurd places. The flowers of course make no such distinction as they're carefully tended and bloom boldly all the year round in their brazen Spanish style – no sign of timorous wallflowers over here! Big, bright, primary colours, some in the shape of hummingbirds and twice the size, others huge trumpets so big and long that they can't hold their own weight and slowly drag their own hosting plant down to its knees, others so numerous that they're clambering over each other in the fight for survival. We even have an all-year-round freshwater spring about 20 metres from our front door. I take our plastic containers and fill them at the ever-flowing supply of running water which spouts out of the rock-face.

And me? Who or what am I? Well, I'm an observer, a blow-in, an outsider, a recorder of events, I watch life and I write and compose music about it, and what better place to make music than here?

Except for the barking of dogs in the distance and the occasional hum of a passing car, there's nothing much to distract me from my professional daydreaming, I can pick up my guitar at any time and work on a new song, or maybe pace around with my penny whistle, teaching my poor little fingers new tricks and new tunes, always pausing by the balcony… until I come to again, realizing another five minutes has passed me by.

Anyway what will be, will be. Then it's off to work, yes I do actually work! Every night you can hear me in the hotels, playing soft music whilst people dine and livening it up a little when they feel in the mood to dance. It's a pleasant way to pass an evening. Yes, life's certainly grand in Gran Canaria!

Elsa Jean McTaggart, www.mctaggart.info

TOWN AND COUNTRY GUIDE

"How can you leave weather like this?" Friends
disapprove of our plans for an English holiday. It was
the first sunny day we'd had in Las Palmas in a month.
They weren't joking.

NORTH GRAN CANARIA

There's a definite north-south divide on the island. Grey,
miserable days occur in the north where in the south they're
the exception that proves the southern results rule when
it comes to weather. Perhaps this explains how the south
cornered the tourism market. Initially, travellers flocked
to Las Palmas with Agatha Christie an early visitor. Las
Palmas photographer and journalist Alex Bramwell's
convinced the capital can reclaim tourists if it works on
its brand image: "Las Palmas deserves to be known as the
Habana of Europe and should be promoted as a city break
destination in its own right."

Yet Las Palmas is but one of seven northern boroughs.
There are the coastal municipalities aka the north coast of
Arucas, Galdar and Santa María de Guía. These areas gear
themselves more towards agriculture although they're
developing more than a passing interest in tourism.

Arucas lies closest to Las Palmas. Prior to the 1980s the
cash crop was the banana. However, plantations have

tailed off since then due to a combination of factors which include increased labour costs and water shortage. The *platano* has survived in Gáldar however with 90% of bananas now grown in the region along with the municipality's distinctive red onions. Meanwhile, Santa María de Guía relies heavily on horticulture. San Juan hosts the most lettuce crops in the area whilst Santa Cristina is rather more noted for its carrots and potatoes.

Further inland, you'll find Firgas, Moya and Teror. The first two are staking a claim to the growing eco-tourist market with their surfeit of hiking and mountain-biking routes. Teror meanwhile remains the most important destination for religious visitors, a sort of Mecca and Jerusalem rolled into one.

Arucas

A is for Arucas, a lovely place dubbed *the "pearl of Gran Canaria"*. Best approached along the picturesque C-813 which joins A (Arucas) with B (Bañaderos), ditch your wheels in the municipal car park adjoining the Gaudiesque church, *Iglesia de San Juan Bautista*. For Arucas is best explored on foot with its pedestrianized streets offering probably the most relaxed stroll on the whole island.

Warm up on a cold day (it's the north, they do occur) with *churros*. These are Spain's take on a doughnut, longer and thinner than you're probably used to, dipped into an accompanying cup of hot chocolate. They're made to share.

Arucas began life as Arehucas or even Arehuc. This is what the original Canary Islanders called it before the 15th-century Spanish Invasion. The triumphant conquerors who wiped out the local population in 1479 renamed their new settlement, based on the site of the original one, Arucas in 1503.

Beaches

Officially Arucas has five beaches. Yet two of these are actually *charcos*, natural swimming pools, and another is rocky nudist sunbathing area, *Las Salinas*. The remaining two are proper *playas*, the dark magic of *El Puertillo* and the sometimes sandy, sometimes stony *San Andrés.*

Food

Head to the hills for *Casa Brito* (*Calle Pasaje Ter* 17; 928 62 23 23; www.casabrito.com) in Visvique, on the road to Teror for a thrill with your grill. We certainly got a shock when our *jamón*-loving middle son, Alex, ordered a plate of Spain's finest and it turned up on the bill later, priced closer to €20 than we'd have estimated for a portion of ham. Marginally closer to the town-centre, *Meson de la Montaña* (*Montaña de Arucas S/N*; 928 60 08 44; www.mesonarucas.es) is a family favourite on Sunday lunchtime. The buffet offers an excellent introduction to traditional Canarian cuisine, and you can buy tomatoes from the kitchen for young ones to feed the lizards in the restaurant garden.

Accommodation

The four-star rural hotel *La Hacienda del Buen Suceso* (*Carretera de Bañaderos Km1*; 928 62 29 45; www.haciendabuensuceso.com) despite its location next to a working banana plantation provides a chance to get away from it all. Unless they're hosting a wedding that is, which tends to disturb the tranquility like somebody rippling the water of a fishbowl. 18 rooms small, the Hacienda manages to be both cosy and elegant.

Nightlife

Latin sounds abound at the out-of-town *Paladium* (*San Francisco Javier* 47; 600 54 60 89; www.discopaladium.es) although there are regular special nights taking in other styles of music.

Fiestas

24th June unites Arucas in celebration of its patron saint, *San Juan Bautista*. The whole family dress in traditional Canarian clothing which looks like they're recreating an episode of *Heidi*. As they dance along to folk music in a bonfire-lit panorama.

Attractions

Destilerías Arehucas, the rum distillery (*Lugar Era de San Pedro* 2, 928 62 49 00; www.arehucas.es) opens it doors to the public from 10 am to 2 pm Monday to Friday. Enjoy a free guided tour and choice of samples at the bar. Then try, yet ultimately fail, to leave without buying a souvenir bottle.

> "This place is unique. 10 minutes from the city, next to the beach and in the country too." Ex-team-mate Oliver sums up why he lives in Bañaderos.

Bañaderos

Prepare to be initially underwhelmed by this north-coast town. We certainly were on our first visit. I'd just enrolled on the *auxiliaries de conversacion* project, a programme which employed native English-language speakers to assist primary-school teachers, and planned on taking a sneak peek at where I'd be working. A particularly windy day didn't lift my spirits much but instead elevated the abundant rubbish on the rundown streets.

Fast forward three years and we're seriously considering relocating there. Five years and we're celebrating our eldest son's first communion at its *El Puertillo* restaurant. Well, what happened? Bañaderos has certainly tarted itself up somewhat. We'd also yet to discover what has become one of our favourite beaches, *El Puertillo*. Nor had we found the *Plaza de San Pedro*, the town's main square, another of Bañaderos' hidden gems.

Beaches

The sooty sand of *El Puertillo*'s a hit with families. Fellow expat Susan (Susana to her Canarian friends) explains why size is important: "With two young kids it's much easier for me to keep my eye on them here than if we

were at a bigger beach like Las Canteras in Las Palmas.".
And unlike at *Canteras*, you won't struggle to locate a
parking space.

Food

Visit south-side Bañaderos for *Bar La Fundada* (*Plaza
de San Pedro* 2; 928 62 78 88). Offering home cooking
delivered with a modern flourish, it's as kind to your
wallet as it's to your palate. Over on the north side of
the GC-2, *Restaurante El Puertillo* (*Paseo Marítimo del
Puertillo* 12; 928 62 75 37), the self-styled *Balcon de
Atlantico*, is a popular draw – not least for the welcoming
hospitality provided by the Hormiga family. As well as the
freshest fish, there are any number of vegetarian dishes
including *croquetas de gofio y berros*, toasted cornflour
and watercress croquettes, *paella vegetariana*, and *papas
arrugadas*, boiled baby potatoes cooked in salty water
served with *mojo*, a piquant sauce typically prepared with
cumin, coriander, parsley, and olive oil.

Accommodation

Despite rumours of new hotels, courtesy of the multi-
million development of this stretch of the north coast,
the closest current places to stay are in Las Palmas and
neighbouring Arucas.

Nightlife

A residential area rather than a tourist resort, the majority
of the bars close at midnight when most of Bañaderos are
already safely ensconced in bed.

Fiestas

The *Fiestas de San Pedro Apostol*, held in honour of Bañaderos' patron saint, extend from the middle of June to the start of July. A curious mishmash of the sacred and the secular, they range from solemn religious processions to thrilling motocross events.

Attractions

The area's redevelopment appears to be suffering somewhat at the hands of the credit crunch, so the scheduled dolphinarium may be delayed. Ditto the golf course. Yet our family love it just the way it is and we challenge you to feel differently.

Firgas knows exactly where it's at

Firgas

I first encountered Firgas on a balmy July evening having been sent there to cover a *lucha canaria* fight night. Arriving on the back of the photogapher's motorbike, its whitewashed buildings lit up by a new moon were a delight after the holding-on-for-grim-life journey. Yet my second visit in daylight hours, following a more sedate ride in the car, was an altogether flatter experience. Famous for its production of sparking mineral water (200,000 bottles a day) which sells under the same name, surprisingly Firgas lacks fizz. Nevertheless it's a nice enough place to break up a drive around the island. Check out the *paseos de Canaria* and *de Gran Canaria*, where a man-made waterfall shoots *agua* 30 metres down shallow steps, on your walk on the mild side.

Founded in 1488 by the new colonials, Firgas' name derives from the *canarii Afurgad* meaning both 'crossroads' and 'high place'. The man most instrumental in its early Spanish history was one Tomás Rodríguez de Palenzuela. A Burgos-born archer with experience of fighting Arabs, Tommy Boy channelled his energies into constructing a irrigation ditch which utilized the natural springs to aid the nascent sugar-cane industry.

Beaches
Located 20 kilometres inland from Las Palmas and a winding 30-minute drive by car, Firgas unsurprisingly has no beaches to speak of.

Food

Fertile Firgas is the perfect place to grow every Canarian's favourite greens, *berros* (watercress). Sample the traditional *potaje de berros* (watercress stew) at a host of local restaurants, the pick of which is arguably the *Asadero Las Brasas* (*Avenida de la Cruz 36;* 928 62 52 50; www.lasbrasas.net). Napkins are essential wear here for the curiously-monikered *pollo escarranchao* (spreadeagled chicken) and *chuletas de cerdo* (pork chop) because of the obvious risk of splashback.

Accommodation

980 metres above sea level, you'll find the three-star *Hotel y Albergue Rural Doramas* (*Montaña de Firgas* 1; 928 61 62 50; www.fondadoramas.com). Breathe in the genuine fragrance of eucalyptus, as the tree is native to this region, in accommodation that's more about rest and relaxation than rock and roll. My brother-in-law Mario introduced me to this establishment on one of our irregular Sunday family get-togethers.

Nightlife

More a pub than a club kind of place, dress down rather than up for a night out in Firgas.

Fiestas

Freud would have had a field day if he'd observed events that go on the 11th August. Here, as part of the *Fiestas de San Roque,* held in honour of the town's patron saint, there's the Descent of the Pole (*Traída del Palo*). Locals travel down from the mountain carrying a long, cylindrical piece of wood which is later, 'wink', erected in the centre and used to raise the municipal flag.

Attractions

Meet Firgas' answer to Windy Miller at the 16th-century *Molino del Conde*. He'll show you how to grind the traditional *gofio* and then invite you to try some. To savour the real Gran Canaria, you should take him up on his offer.

Gáldar

When we first moved to Gran Canaria, I was a house husband looking after our lovely boy Alex who had been diagnosed with leukaemia as a baby. His doctor over here advised while he couldn't go to nursery with other children; he'd recommend the beach. Now my mother-in-law's got a seaside apartment in Las Palmas, but seeing as I'm somewhat LP-phobic, I ventured out of the capital at every available opportunity. Which explains how we we found ourselves at Gáldar bus station waiting for a connection to what remains my favourite little bit of shoreline, *Sardina del Norte*. It's a bus station we've revisited many times since. And not only to return to Sardina, but to take time out in Gran Canaria's most perfect square, the laurel-shaded *Plaza de Santiago*.

Beaches

Of the seven beaches you'll find in and around Galdar, two stand out as must-sees. *Sardina del Norte*'s the destination of choice for bodyboarders, divers and those looking for a quiet break (my wife remarked on her first visit, "It's like being on holiday"). You'll need a 4x4 to negotiate the way to *Juncal* before a steep footpath leads to one of Gran Canaria's best-kept secrets.

Food

You'll find the two best restaurants in Gáldar in Sardina del Norte. Enter an anonymous-looking bar at *La Cueva* (*Avenída Alcalde Antonio Rosas* 80; 928 88 02 36) to discover the treasure within: a stylish restaurant housed in a cave. Further along what passes for a promenade in Sardina, you'll reach *Restaurante La Fragata* (*Avenída Alcalde Antonio Rosas S/N*; 928 88 32 96; where Alex goes all feline on us by feasting on the freshest sardines liberally doused in lemon juice.

Accommodation

Shake off the dust of the approach road at the clean and serene *Hacienda de Anzo* (*Vega de Anzo S/N*; 928 55 16 55; www.haciendadeanzo.20m.com). With just six rooms, you're guaranteed a quiet stay at this three-star converted mansion. And on a clear day from the terraces, you'll even be able to make out the neighbouring island of Tenerife.

Nightlife

The bars in and around the *Plaza de Santiago* offer outside tables to drink even after the sun goes down.

Fiestas

Arm yourselves with, erm, floral weapons at the famous *batalla de flores* (battle of flowers) which engulfs the *Plaza de Santiago* and surrounding areas on the 25th July each year. This friendly fight occurs during the *Fiesta de Santiago de los Caballeros*, the party held in honour of the town's patron saint, James the Apostle.

Attractions

For a fun introduction to archaeology, visit *El Museo y Parque Arqueológico Cueva Pintada* (*Calle Audiencia 2*; 928 89 57 46; www.cuevapintada.com), the Painted Cave Museum and Archaelogical Park, well-signposted from your arrival in Gáldar. Offering guided tours in English, French, German, and Spanish, don x-ray specs to watch a fascinating recreation of pre-Spanish history on the island.

"Your face's longer than a horse," man pretending to jockey an ostrich fails to get me in the carnival mood.

Las Palmas

All Made Up – Carnival Queens strut their stuff

At a reception at the plush *Hotel Santa Catalina* to welcome the new British Ambassador Denise Holt back in 2007, I got cornered by a fellow expat who was moaning about the road from the airport to Las Palmas. "They should do something about it, it's just so depressing," she said.

I nodded in agreement, in fact, my brother, on his first visit, had genuinely enquired "Is there a war on?" before adding that for me the most depressing thing was that it led to Las Palmas. The shocked expat gulped and moved on to talk to somebody more pro-LP.

They say it takes time for Las Palmas to get under your skin but when it does, you're hooked. Well, I'm still waiting. Yet, I know I'm a hypocrite. One of the things I miss most about living in the UK is London. And here I am residing in Spain's seventh-biggest city but hankering for a home on or around the less-populated north coast. But if I have to live in Las Palmas, which I do for work, I can't fault the area I live in much, Arenales. It's within walking distance of the vaguely historic centre and our academy, which is handy as I still haven't learned to drive. I got round London on foot and public transport, and it hasn't changed being over here.

Athens, Barcelona, Copenhagen, Florence, Istanbul, Las Palmas, Paris, Rome, Seville: all cities featuring the distinctive red *City Sightseeing* buses. It's easy enough to spot the odd one out. I was once commissioned by local paper *RTN Canarias* to write a first-person narrative of this bus tour and pointed out that it was ironically titled as there aren't any sights to see.

Of course I'm using hyperbole to make a point. Although fellow journalist Alex Bramwell suggests Las Palmas marketing itself as a short-haul Havana. And not only because LP's *Avenída Maritima* bears some sort of resemblance to Havana's famous *Malecon*.

Take time out to explore the largely-pedestrianized *Vegueta*, the old town. Here you'll find the pick of the museums and churches, including the *Catedral Santa Ana*. Similarly walker-friendly neighbouring Triana serves as the main shopping district, pity though you have to cross a main road from Vegueta to reach it.

Beaches

I used to accompany my sons Alex and Dani on their bikes to *Alcaravaneras*, the portside beach that's the nearest stretch of swimmable water to our Las Palmas home. With the wind on our side haring along the *Avenída Maritima*, we were door to shore in ten minutes. Then Dani started to complain about the local drunks having vocal, and sometimes physical, arguments on the beach. And I noticed they'd built a homeless centre next to the ramshackle bar at the *Club Nautico* end. In truth, the beach's proximity to our residence had been the only factor in its favour. Personally, I'd tired of feeling the sludge of oil on my feet from the adjacently-moored yachts and missed the roar of the nearby *Canteras*. Although fellow parents rave about the beach because of its lack of waves which they claim makes it more kid-friendly.

Now when we go out on our bikes, we head south on the *AM* rather than north. Passing through the pretty former fishing village of San Cristóbal, now sadly a suburb of Las Palmas, we end up at *La Laja*. You won't find homeless shelters and public drunkenness here. Although Laja does has its downsides too. It's right next to the GC-1 motorway, so it's not a (sea) garden of serenity by any means. And whilst its strong currents draw water-sports enthusiasts, it's not the safest beach for younger children.

But if we're feeling lazy or Dani wants to go surfing, we jump on the bus and head to *Las Canteras* – Las Palmas' main beach. Stretching from the rough-and-ready *Cicer*, the surfer's choice, to the more refined, nay dull, *La*

Puntilla, Las Canteras is undoubtedly one of the world's great urban beaches. *Cicer* lies next door to the traditionally working-class area of *Guanarteme,* which has received a fair bit of recent investment whilst *La Puntilla* fronts the similarly blue-collar *La Isleta* which has received less.

Continue past *La Puntilla* however and you'll eventually end up at *El Confital*. Home to competitive surfers and naturists, this blue-flag beach transports you away from the hustle and bustle of Las Palmas. To an altogether more serene place where children can explore the rock pools and you can reconnect with nature.

Food

Along with the southern resorts, Las Palmas's the place where you'll discover the greatest variety of restaurants on the island. Unsurprisingly, the fruits of the sea feature heavily on the menus of restaurants specializing in Canarian cuisine and even those that don't, here Chinese restaurants feature real seaweed on their menus rather than the cabbage substitute offered in Chinatowns worldwide. There are also Japanese and Korean restaurants for lovers of Asian food.

Bar Rosmi (*Paseo de las Canteras 43*; 928 22 54 77) with a menu 11 entries short, nevertheless offers a more authentic introduction to Asian cuisine (in this case Korean) than the Chinese buffet eateries littering the rest of the promenade above *Canteras* beach. Nearby, you'll find the exception proving the rule that it's impossible to find a good vegetarian restaurant in Las Palmas: *Bambu*

(*Paseo de las Canteras* 63; 928 22 25 74). Old staples seitan and tofu dominate the menu but they're sexed up beyond belief by a dynamic chef who even managed to make a starter that I ordered, which was essentially a plate of spinach, one of the most mouthwatering dishes I've ever enjoyed.

For something completely different, there's *El Rincón Los Nidillos* (*Calle Valsendero S/N*; 928 46 29 01) which attracts a loyal *La Isleta* following. If you're lucky, you'll catch an impromptu concert. If not, you can still savour ocean-fresh seafood and sun-warm service.

When in *Triana*, head to *La Alquitara* (*Calle Domingo J. Navarro* 9; 928 38 49 59; www.laalquitara.es). Ignore the tacky pictures of food which ´adorn´ the restaurant's exterior. For the tasting menu, lovingly crafted by head chef and owner Emilio J. Cabrera López, is one of the most imaginative on the island and if you can't find a decent wine to accompany it; you're obviously not looking hard enough, given there are close to 1,200 labels to choose from. Fusing Basque-Country cooking with Canarian cuisine, *La Alquitaria*'s a temple to cod – with said fish appearing in no less than 18 dishes on the set menu. No wonder there's an international shortage.

Elsewhere, *San Cristóbal* boasts the finest concentration of excellent restaurants in the capital. *La Sama*, where Flamenco dancer Joaquin Cortes famously romanced supermodel Naomi Campbell, may have gone but fixtures like *Restaurante Chacalote* (*Calle Proa* 3; 928 31 21 40;

www.restaurantechacalote.net) remain. Augmented by relative newcomer *El Cucharón* (*Calle Marina 5*; 928 33 13 65; www.elcucharon.es) overlooking the historic *Castillo de San Cristóbal*, where locals congregate to collect cockles and whelks, and old favourite *Los Botes* (*Calle Timonel* 43; 928 33 27 28) with sea-fronting terrace, it's impossible to go hungry in *San Cristóbal*.

Accommodation

Fit for a king, the five-star *Hotel Santa Catalina* is the hotel of choice when Spanish royalty deigns to visit the island (*Calle León y Castillo* 227; 928 24 30 40; www.hotelsantacatalina.com). For beachside luxury, don't look beyond four-star *Hotel Reina Isabel* (*Calle Alfredo L. Jones* 40; 928 26 01 00; www.bullhotels.com/ reinaisabel) enjoying a suitably regal position on the *Canteras* promenade. On the other side of town, located in arguably Las Palmas' loveliest street, *Calle Perojo* where properties are painted in various shades of pastel, you'll find your best budget option. Clean and with young friendly staff, a stay at *Pensión Perojo* (*Calle Perojo* 1; 928 37 13 87) comes with only one problem – its location at the noisier Bravo Murillo end of the street.

Nightlife

Its success may have hit its bohemian reputation but it's still worth checking out late-night hangout *Charleston Café* (*Calle Buenos Aires* 14; 928 37 24 92; www.charlestoncafe.info), one of the only bars on the island to stock absinthe and a concert venue positively encouraging audience participation. Open to 3.30 am

Monday through to Sunday, its central location close to *Parque San Telmo* means it's the perfect start or end of a pub crawl. *Vegueta*, a brisk 5-minute walk/leisurely 10-minute stroll away is the oldest part of town but at night it attracts the young and young at heart who flood its numerous bars and clubs. For a more relaxed option, head out of town to *Las Brujas* (*Barranco Seco S/N*; 639 71 74 74; www.lasbrujas.net), a converted 16th-century mansion and a joy to tour, drink in hand.

Fiestas

Celebrations come and go in Las Palmas, almost it seems on a weekly basis, but nothing touches *Carnaval* for popularity. Featuring more cross-dressing than at a *Little Britain* convention, the emphasis is on the costume. Forget the food, drink and music, I once heard Tom Jones' *Delilah* pumping non-ironically out of some speakers. Each year, organizers arrange carnival around a theme. Dates vary but it usually starts sometime in January/February and ends sometimes in February/March. For further details, check out www.lpacarnaval.com.

Attractions

For a reduced cultural tour of Las Palmas, you won't even need to leave *Vegueta*. Start at futuristic art gallery, *CAAM* (*Calle Los Balcones* 11, 928 31 18 00; www.caam.net). The *Centro Atlántico de Arte Moderno* offers a rolling schedule of free exhibitions by African, South American and Spanish artists.

Before stepping back in time with a visit to *Casa de Colón* (*Calle Colón* 1; 928 312 373; www.casadecolon.com), a museum dedicated to the discovery of America by Christopher Columbus housed in his residence during his time in LP. Another historic building worth exploring is the emblematic *Catedral de Santa Ana.* 400 years in the making, it's proved to be well worth the wait.

> "I've never seen a place quite like El Roque before or since. The lime-white cottages clustered tight in medieval fashion on either side of a six-foot-wide stone path that twisted and roller-coasted up and down, following the idiosyncrasies of the promontory's rocky top. I passed a couple of shops the size of broom closets that doubled as rum bars for the men. Crusty bronzed faces peered out curiously from shadowy doorways. Old women, shrouded in black, scurried by." Travel writer David Yeadon remembers a 20th-century visit to Gran Canaria's north coast. It hasn't changed much since.

Moya

The first time I chanced upon Moya was on a stretch-your-legs stop-off on a tour of the island with the *Pequeño Valiente* charity who help families with children suffering from cancer. My wife Cristina is the president. I didn't think much of it but repeating the trip with my parents I coerced them into getting out there for my daily caffeine fix of a *cortado largo*, an espresso cut with a spurt of milk. We left soon after with my folks remarking that you *literally* shouldn't go out of your way to visit Moya. Moya actually looks more attractive approaching than when you arrive. Travelling on the GC-700 from lowly Guía, check out the stunning vista of the ravine-hugging *Iglesia de Nuestra Señora de la Candelaria*. It's also a great base to explore the surrounding area which includes a 1.8km footpath through *Los Tilos de Moya*, one of the last surviving laurel-tree forests on the island.

This settlement founded by the Spanish was previously unoccupied by the *canarii* who nonetheless treasured the rich fertile region to the north which they called *Agunastel*. It was here that one of the last of their tribe, the brave Doramas, used to be roam. In tribute to him, the area of outstanding natural beauty which includes Los Tilos is named *Parque Rural de Doramas*.

Beaches

La Caleta de Moya is popular with the surf crowd whilst *Charco de San Lorenzo*, a natural swimming pool, is only worth visiting when the tide is low. Else a relaxed paddle becomes an extreme sport. Repeat, definitely not child-friendly when the tide is high.

Food
Those with a sweet tooth won't be able to leave Moya without stocking up on its famous *bizcochos*. These sponge fingers by any other name are perfect for dunking into a nightime glass of milk for a late-night snack. There's not much way of good places to eat in the town itself, so head for its coastal outpost and *Locanda El Roque* (*El Roque* 58; 928 61 00 44; www.locandaelroque.com), an adventurous Italian restaurant that features an oceanside terrace. For a weekend visit, book in advance as otherwise you'll be met by a waiting list. We pitched up one Sunday and found ourselves number 14 on the list – needless to add, we missed out on a lunch with a view that day.

Accommodation
Hotels are rather thin on ground in Moya. Consider hiring out a holiday home instead. Located 1km from the town centre, *Casa Rural El Drago* (*Camino de Moreto* 1; 600 31 73 96; www.casarural-eldrago.com) is an excellent base for hiking.

Nightlife
Dodo-dead at night, Moya's not the place to paint the town red.of le

Fiestas
Take the time out to visit the *Iglesia de Nuestra Señora de la Candelaria* and you'll see a figure of the Virgin of

Candelaria crafted out of cedar. Further homage to this, the patron saint of Moya, is paid on the weekend that falls closest to the 2nd February. As well as a floral offering, there are two evenings' worth of traditional musical entertainment.

Attractions

Apart from the church, the other place of interest in Moya is the *Casa-Museo Tomás Morales* (*Plaza de Tomás Morales S/N*, 928 62 02 17; www.tomasmorales.com). Facing the *Iglesia*, it houses the home in which the modernist poet's modernist poet was born, back on 10th November 1884. View Morales' first typewriter and manuscripts, alongside other Morales memorabilia.

San Andrés

José, Reyes and their daughter Julía are good friends of ours from Vecindario. Come August when the majority of Las Palmas migrate to the warmer climes of the south, they make the reverse journey. To San Andrés and peace or "*tranquilidad*" as Reyes tells me whilst adopting the guru stance.

In truth, there's not a lot to do in ´San An´ as nobody else calls it. Which is its appeal to José and co. Everybody needs to switch off sometimes.

Most people bypass San Andrés on their way to Gáldar, Agaete and beyond. Having not long left Las Palmas, they think it's too soon to stop. But to whiz on by is the very antithesis of Canarian life, after all locals make the sloth look the very epitome of busy.

Beaches
One of the most curious beaches on the island, *Playa San Andrés* changes composition during the course of the year. From sandy to stony and back again. 450m long, it's the biggest of the Arucas beaches, and a popular surfing venue with breaks including *Molokai* and *Los Enanos* to enable you to get up, stand up.

Food
While you won't exactly go hungry in San Andrés for lack of choice, better restaurants are to be found in neighbouring Bañaderos, El Altillo and Gáldar.

Accommodation
San Andrés is too small to sustain a hotel, so consider nearby Arucas instead.

Nightlife
The nocturnal scene at San Andrés consists of a barbecue soundtracked by the sound of breaking waves.

Fiestas
Where Scotland celebrate their patron saint on the 28th November, the good people of San Andrés extend their *fiestas patronales* from the 21st to the 29th November. It's not that Canarians are workshy, okay it's not only that Canarians are workshy. It's just that they don't have to look hard for an excuse to party.

Attractions

A pleasant main square boasting a handsome church is worth visiting in August when a giant screen comes to San Andrés bringing with it free cinema. Ordinarily it's nothing you'd consider worth paying for, just as well there's no cover charge then. To the west of the village lies the *Barranco de la Virgen*. This riverbank is notoriously dry, to the extent locals have built a football pitch on it. And on the couple of days a year the river fills; well there's always water polo.

San Felipe

One Halloween, I partied below the picturesque bridge on the GC-2 that looms over the village of San Felipe – alongside what appeared to be extras from Michael Jackson's famous *Thriller* video. Although I hadn't bothered to dress up for the occasion, I had a tip-top time – burgeoning the love affair I'd already embarked upon with the north of the island.

It wasn't until a later date that I actually saw San Felipe itself. My sister-in-law's husband's family (and if you think that's a mouthful in English, consider the Spanish alternative: *la familia del hombre de mi cuñada*) have a house there, which they use as a bolthole from their Las Palmas residence on weekends. Knowing I was vegetarian, the mother of the family plonked down a salad comprising beetroot, potato, onion and egg tossed in a vinaigrette (a recipe which I've tried but consistently failed to replicate) in front of me – the warmest of welcomes for my eternally-hungry stomach.

San Felipe came to my tummy's rescue again when we were struggling to find a restaurant to celebrate Christmas Day with my parents who were over for the occasion. All our favourites were either closed or fully booked. Which bemused my wife and I somewhat as traditionally Canarian families consider the Christmas Eve dinner to be more important. I'd heard of a weird Canarian-Moroccan hybrid that had opened next to San Felipe's beach and because we didn't have a lot of other options, we schlepped all the way there. And to our relief, *El Rifeño* was open.

Beaches
The defiantly non-swimming-friendly *Pagador* and *San Felipe* beaches are the warts of the north coast, ugly to look at but functional in that they serve the surfing community.

Food
The aforementioned *El Rifeño* (*Barrio de San Felipe* 74; 928 55 61 62; www.actiweb.es/elrifeno) is the place to go for *pinchos* and is veggie-friendly too. Rather less so is *Bar La Tasquita* (Barrio de San Felipe 32; 928 55 63 83),

All members of staff are English-speaking. although they did improvise a relatively exciting salad, well by Gran Canaria's unexacting standards anyway. My wife had booked a birthday meal there on a recommendation. On arriving at a soporific bar, she exclaimed, "This can't be it!" But we were yet to discover the charming garden and its tables boasting excellent views of the Atlantic.

Accommodation

The only real place to stay is the *San Felipe Surf House* which offers a reasonable rate for both surfers and non-surfers, on a weekly basis. For further details, visit www.soulridercamp.com/europe/canary-islands/gran-canaria/packages/surf-drive/san-felipe-only-accomodation.

Nightlife

The bright lights of Las Palmas are a a mere blip of a 15-minute drive away.

Fiestas

San Felipe forms part of the municipality of Santa María de Guía which is famous for its *papahuevos*. View these fancy-dress costumes with their freaky giant papier-mâché heads at the fiesta celebrating San Felipe's patron saint. On the 30th May each year.

Attractions

Less is more in San Felipe. Enjoy the silence. Lovers of noise can head on east to LP.

Santa María de Guía

Known by those in the know as simply Guía and separated from rival Gáldar by the GC-2, there's some confusion over which municipality owns what. For example, Becerril and La Atalaya are both on the Gáldar side of the motorway, but belong to SMDG. It was easier when they were one and the same place but Guía tired of big brother Gáldar and opted for independence.

Architecture is not Gran Canaria's strong point but Guía enjoyed a moneyed early history. Its first settlers included wealthy Genoese bankers and merchants. They left an enduring present in the 17th-century *Casa de los Quintana*, whose stunning wooden balcony was enjoyed by the town's original mayor.

Also located in the pretty old town is the *Parroquia de Santa María de Guía*. This parish church's neoclassical façade fronts a baroque interior featuring altarpieces by local sculptor, José Luján Pérez. Poet Graciliana Afonso was even commissioned to write a sonnet in praise of the church's bell.

Beaches

A rocky coast includes two hidden gems. Head on down from La Atalaya to *Roque Prieto* for a beautiful natural pool – where Alex learned to swim. Even more out of the way, as in no mobile coverage, is *Caleta Arriba* where Alex saw, or at least noticed, fishermen for the first time.

Food

Gastronomically speaking, Guía's famous for its *queso de flor*, flower cheese. Made by curdling the milk of the cow, or more typically goat, with the head of the *cardo azul* (blue thistle), it's then stored in caves which lends it a distinctive taste. *La Quesera* (*Calle Medico Estevez* 3; 928 55 33 26) caters for those crackers about cheese and offers a strict try-before-you-buy policy.

Accommodation

Guía's youth hostel *Albergue Juvenil San Fernando* (*Avenída de la Juventud S/N*; 928 88 36 81) represents your best bet for a budget stay in the area. Another, albeit pricier, option is *Los Escobones* (*Barranco del Pilar* 18, Montaña Alta; 646 27 39 38; www.losescobones.com), a *casa rural* in the *Parque Doramas* featuring a wealth of signposted walks to enjoy.

Nightlife

Ssh, don't tell anyone, and amble over to the other side of the GC-2 and Gáldar for a livelier nocturnal scene.

Fiestas

Vegans should give Guía a wide berth during late April and early May. For this is when the province hosts the *Fiestas del Queso*. Held in alternate years in either Guía town centre or Montaña Alta, you'll be able to smell the festivities before you see them.

Attractions

Anybody with an interest in archaelogy will, I apologize in advance, dig the *Cenobio de Valeron* (*Cuesta de Silva S/N;*.618 60 78 96; www.cenobiodevaleron.com). A spectacular granary housed in volcanic rock, it predates the Spanish conquest. Take a guided tour or discover its minor joys by yourself.

Teror

Steeped in history, the locals even use the traditional springs of Teror's *fuente agria* to draw water from. Elsewhere, you have to pay for *Agua de Teror*. This rivals *Aguas Minerales de Firgas* as the most popular mineral water on home and restaurant tables. The island's religious centre, Teror is well worth making a pilgrimage to. The *Basílica de Nuestra Señora del Pino* located in the square of the same name positively demands your attention. The grand 18th-century three-naved church also houses a statue of the *Virgen de Pino*, the patron saint of the Canaries.

Walk through Teror's pedestranized streets and if you get the impression you're being spied on, you're not being paranoid. For the traditional wooden balconies make perfect vantage points for inquisitive Canarians who count people-watching as one of their favourite pastimes.

Beaches

I grew up in Nottingham, a city reknowned for being one of the furthest away from the sea. Hence, every summer they rename the Old Market Square the *Nottingham Riveira* and cover it with 300 tonnes of sand and 600 metres of boardwalk. It's an experiment they could replicate in the similarly landlocked Teror, but probably won't.

Food

Teror is not so far from the beach however that prevents its restaurants from offering fish dishes, with the traditional *sancocho* (sea bass stew) a fixture on most menus. Try it at the *El Rincon de Magüi* (*Calle de la Diputación* 6; 928 63 04 54) which also caters for the Canarian love of pizza. For an *alfresco* introduction to tapas, look no further than *La Villa* (*Plaza Nuestra Señora del Pino* 7; 928 63 26 07) whose outdoor tables offer the perfect setting for a leisurely lunch.

Accommodation

Best explore Teror on a day trip, although you could sleep over at *Hotel J.M El Pino* (*Avenída del Cabildo Insular* 141; 928 63 20 16), a two-star establishment located closer to the Finca de Osorio and its 207 hectares of natural beauty than the town-centre. For a more central stay, there's always *Casa Rural Doña Margarita* (*Calle Padre Cueto* 4; 609 62 90 76; www.margaritacasarural.com). Its elegant 18th-century building houses three separate living spaces to rent.

Nightlife

When the sun turns in for the night, so does the populace.

Fiestas

The main fiesta's the *Fiesta en Honor de Nuestra Señora del Pino*. On September 8th each year, people walk from Las Palmas or Tamaraceite, to bring offerings to the saint. But when you reach Teror, there's as much secular shenanigans as spiritual reverence with anybody wielding a *timple* (a Canarian pygmy guitar) usually orchestrating a singalong.

Attractions

Apart from the obvious, yes, that great big basilica which dominates the Teror skyline, check out the *Casa de los Patronos de la Virgen* (*Plaza Nuestra Señora del Pino* 8; 928 63 02 39). The town's only museum smells like the musty libraries of my childhood. The story it has to tell however is an altogether different one; of the Canarian artistocracy's lifestyle of years gone by.

> *"Panza de burro?* More like *culo de pero." Exasperated expat Sam Cash rechristens Las Palmas' summer-long cloud* "the dog's arse."

EAST GRAN CANARIA

As well as a north-south divide, there's a definite split between east and west. If it's cloudy in the east, which it often is, it's clear in the west. And if it's cloudy in the west, you can't be reading your compass correctly.

The *panza de burro* extends to the east as well as north. Hardest hit, of course, is Las Palmas by virtue of its north-east location. Although, as I've had the discomfort of discovering, you can still get sunburnt even if there isn't any sun in the sky.

The east of the island is the first thing you'll see as you get off the plane. This has given it a whole load of image problems. Some of which are obviously unfair as airports are intended to be functional rather than striking.

Gran Canaria's *aeropuerto* has LPA as its airport code. Which is confusing as it lies not in the municipality of Las Palmas but Telde. The centre of which is an undervisited part of the island for residents, let alone tourists.

Gran Canaria doesn't really do industry, apart from tourism, but the east is the island's industrial heartland. When I complain of the environmental impact on its numerous beaches, Canarians always point out the north coast's agricultural links. Well, personally a beach closer to a farm appeals over one bordering an industrial estate.

Further inland you'll find Agüimes and Valsequillo who wear their history like standard-bearers. Many visitors don't include this pretty pair on their itinerary as they represent a detour. But taking the road less travelled, as famous poet Robert Frost remarked, can make all the difference. Especially as the *canarii* populated the east of Gran Canaria more heavily than any other region – as can be seen by the wealth of aboriginal remains in this area.

Agüimes

Step back in time in ancient (well as ancient as the Canaries get) Agüimes. A beautifully-preserved *casco historico* (old town) dating back to 1486 features low-level traditional Canarian buildings, replete with what looks like pock marks. Look out for the twin towers of the *Parroquia de San Sebastián*, a parish church disguised as a cathedral.

Separated from Ingenio by the *Barranco de Guayadeque*, Agüimes is the first major place of interest you'll reach heading south from the airport. 11km from LPA, you can also use buses 11 and 21 to reach it. Which start at Las Palmas' *San Telmo* bus station but bypass the airport.

Located 500 metres above sea level, make your way to Agüimes' coastal area along what's been dubbed the *Sculpture Promenade*. These works of art further prettify one of Gran Canaria's most gentrified municipalities. A world away from the soulless *centros comerciales*, Agüimes is all heart.

Beaches

Windier than a baked-bean eater's constitution, *Arinaga* enjoys a loyal local following. As does the similarily trade-wind-afflicted, *Balos*. Watersports enthusiasists will enjoy the out-of-the way *Cabrón* (diving) and the easier-to-find *Vargas* (windsurfing) – home of the annual world championship, the *Vargas PWA Wave Classic Grand Prix*.

Food

I once fell onto an *erizo de mar*, a sea urchin, and its spikes remained embedded in my hand until a prolonged one-on-one session with a pair of tweezers. Yet so extensive is the seafood menu at Arinaga's *Restaurante Nelson* (*Avenida Polizón* 47; 928 18 08 60; www.restaurantenelson.com) they even offer a *revuelto con erizos de mar y ajos tiernos* (scrambled eggs with sea urchins and garlic shoots). In downtown Agüimes itself, look no further than *El Oroval* (*Calle Progreso* 12; 928 78 50 03) – the award-winning in-house restaurant of *Casa de Los Camellos*, part of the esteemed *Hecansa* chain of establishments.

Accommodation

In a past life, the aforementioned *Casa de Los Camellos* (*Calle Progreso* 12; 928 78 50 03) was a granary flanked by camel stables. Nowadays, it's a rustic hotel with 12 bedrooms. *Hecansa* have also converted the nearby old town hall into *Hotel Villa de Agüimes* (*Calle Sol* 3; 928 78 50 03). Six bedrooms small, it's a budget version of its larger neighbour.

Nightlife

Located in a nowhere land with regards to clubs, head north to Telde or south, to the major resorts, to get your freak on.

Fiestas

Yet again the parties held in honour of the patron saint are the big draw. In Agüimes, that's the *Fiestas de Nuestra Señora del Rosario*, ordinarily bridging September and October. The highlight of this is the last Saturday of September and the celebration of *Traída del Agua y del Gofio* which recreates the journey from mill to town. Along the 2-km walk, thousands dress up in Canarian costume to fetch *gofio*, the famous roasted grain flour of the island, before they open the sacks in the main square and launch into a food fight with gofio hurled around, coating revellers all and sundry, as the accompanying water tipped from balconies forms a paste that truly binds.

Attractions

Itself a monument to history, it's not surprising that Agüimes is home to one of Gran Canaria's most significant museums. The *Museo de Historia de Agüimes* (*Calle Juan Alvaro y Saz* 42; 928 78 54 53), open Tuesday through to Sunday, dedicates space to the region's aboriginal past, the Spanish conquest, and traditional crafts. Housed in a stately 17th-century mansion, read about the exhibits in English, German, or Spanish.

Ingenio

The *patito feo* (ugly duckling) to its neighbour Agüimes' beautiful swan, Ingenio is not, however, without its own merits. It can boast a historic quarter, which is certainly a respite from the built-up suburbs with their non-postcard views of the airport below. Suburbs which nonetheless include the quirky *finca* owned by my brother-in-law Jorge's father-in-law where the old boy grows, amongst other things, grapes, which he makes into wine, and red onions.

The *Plaza de La Candelaria*'s as good a place as any to commence a tour of Ingenio's old town. Visit the church of the same name, *Iglesia de Candelaria*, an early 20th-century masterpiece built on the remains of the original chapel. Also, check out the *Ayuntamiento de Ingenio*, the town hall and its Swiss-style wooden balcony.

Elsewhere in the centre of town, enjoy the foliage at *Parque Las Mimosas*. In Rome in February flower-sellers sell bunches of mimosa below the Spanish Steps. In this Spanish outpost, you'll see these distinctive yellow flowers in their natural setting.

Beaches

The eternally scruffy *Playa del Burrero* is Ingenio's only beach of any note. Sandy with more than the odd pebble, its combination of strong wind and moderate wave make it a popular draw for sailors and windsurfers alike. Bars and restaurants on the promenade above compete to offer you an Atlantic-view meal.

Food

Pan de puño is the breadbasket-filler of choice on Ingenio dining tables. Made by kneading the dough with your fists (*puños*), it's Ingenio's main gastronomic export. Tourist trap it may well be, but don't let that stop you visiting *Bar Restaurante Tagoror* (*Montaña Las Tierras* 21; 928 17 20 13; www.casasruralesdeguayadeque.com/restaurante-tagoror). You'll find superior-cooked, as well as cheaper, versions of the local favourites on this restaurant's menu elsewhere on the island, but hardly any based in such a stunning setting – a cave no less.

Accommodation

You can probably see all of Ingenio in a day (and that's really dragging it out), so don't bother with a stay. There are better bases to explore the rest of the island from too. Not that there's (m)any lodgings to get down your head at anyway.

Nightlife

You can scarcely dine well in Ingenio, let alone dance.

Fiestas

I once had an argument about bullfighting with a *Madrileño* (thankfully there are no arenas on the Canaries). "Matthew, they love that bull," Mabel insisted. "Before the build-up to the fight, it's granted a life of luxury." Similarly, whilst goat turns up all too regularly on the *cartas* (menus) of Ingenio's restaurants, October's *La Bajá de Macho*, one of the region's most popular *fiestas*, pays tribute to the *Pasadilla Fair*'s best buck.

Attractions

In the build-up to Christmas, everyone and anyone including parks, supermarkets and even hospitals compete to display the most visually-stunning *Belen* (nativity tableau). The *Museo de Piedra y Artesanía Canaria* (*Camino Real de Gando* 1; 928 78 11 24) is no different. This *Canarian Craft and Stone Museum* also allows you to view your souvenirs being made by local artisans.

Telde

Through the oval window - The view from Telde's Basílica San Juan Bautista

Gran Canaria's second city, Telde, was established by papal decree. Way back in 1351. In the past, the surrounding area was a hive of agricultural activity. However, sadly farms and the like have given way to industry, although the city itself retains its history.

Mosey on down to the *San Francisco* area of town for evidence of this. High heels are definitely not the order of the day, unless you want to risk a tumble on the heavily-cobbled streets. Lose yourself in a labyrinth of avenues and alleyways.

Another historic area worth a look at is *San Gregorio*. This is very much Telde's craft centre. At the *Parroquia*

131

de San Gregorio, visit in the morning to beat the crowds, the interior highlights are the neoclassical altarpieces and the carving of the *Virgen de Los Dolores* (Our Lady of the Sorrows).

Beaches
If it wasn't for their industrial backdrop, Telde could claim to have some of the best beaches on the island. Despite that, both *La Garita* and *Melenara* have been proudly flying the blue flag for more successive years than *Las Canteras*, for example. Closer to *El Goro*, *Aguadulce* seems miles away from anyway, although *Tufia*, a popular diving beach, neighbours it.

Food
Where better to enjoy the catch of the day than alongside the person who caught it. Telde's *Cofradia de Pescadores* (*Calle Taliarte S/N*; 928 13 43 87) is handily placed, close to *Playa de Melenara*. The *cofradias de pescadores* are fishermen's guilds which offer fresh-out-of-the-net fruits of the sea at reasonable prices.

Accommodation
You could stay at the *Hotel Rural Cortijo San Ignacio Golf* (*Autopista del Sur GC-1, KM 6,400;* 928 71 24 27; www. cortijosanignaciogolf.com*)*. Consider, however, that's in the over-rated suburb of *El Cortijo*. For a start, it's on the wrong, non-beach side of the motorway and there's the not insubstantial fact of it bordering the unlovely *Jinámar*. A better alternative, and a cheaper one to boot, is *Hostal Albacar* (*Calle Padre Cueto 4*, 928 13 15 20;

www.hostalalbacar.es). Located near *Playa de Melenara*, it offers an opportunity to sample the real Telde rather than the *pjio* (snob) enclave of *El Cortijo*.

Nightlife
Join an older, but still up-for-it, crowd at *Drago II Sala de Fiestas* (*Calle Cruz de Ayala* 8, 928 70 38 67; www.drago2.com). The DJ who seems to have been flown in from South America fills the dancefloor with *reggaeton* and salsa classics. After one or two *cubatas*, it's safer to order *Ron de Telde* here rather than Arehucas, you'll be busting out all your old moves.

Fiestas
Beat the heat in August at the *Fiesta de la Traída del Agua* in Lomo Magullo. Essentially, this involves the liberal dousing of party-goers in H^2O. By the end of the festivities, both boys and girls are sporting wet T-shirts.

Attractions
Started in 1509 but not finished until the 20th century, the imposing *Basílica San Juan Bautista* was a work in progress for what seemed a record amount of years. Push open the heavy wooden door to discover the beauty within. This includes a Jesus figure fashioned out of corn paste by Michoacan Mexicans in 1550.

Valsequillo

At one of my first social events on the island, the birthday party of a friend of a friend in Tafira Alta, I met Raquel, a music teacher. Asking where she worked, she replied in perfect English, seemingly metamorphosing into a wench from the Middle Ages in doing so: "Oh tis a small town, a near-mythical place in the mountains, far, far away from here." I later discovered she was talking about Valsequillo. After such a build-up, an actual visit there was bound to end in crushing disappointment.

And so it turned out. For a start Valsequillo's a mere near-8km away from Tafira Alta. In Raquel's defence, that's as the crow flies, with the choice of road journeys adding on a minimum of 13km. And I did hear another teacher complain about her "almost-suicidal" commute from her Valsequillo home to Las Palmas – the same teacher who told me that if it was hot in Las Palmas, it was hotter in Valsequillo and cold in Las Palmas, colder in her home town.

Despite the inevitable new developments, there's even a gated community (how very North American), Valsequillo has done a lot to preserve its history. The *Cuartel de Colmenar*, constructed in 1530 as a cavalry ballacks, lays claim to the title of Gran Canaria's oldest building. The slumberous old town comes to life on Sunday with the arrival of the market allowing you to buy local, shoulder to shoulder with locals.

Beaches

Located above the airport, Valsequillo lies closest to the beaches of Telde.

Food

The other big centre of cheese on the island, *Quesos Flor Valsequillo* is the local *queso* that dominates fridge space within the major supermarkets in Gran Canaria. There's nothing fancy about the gastronomic scene in Valsequillo. It's comfort food, as can be seen from the home cooking on display at the lilliputian *Bar Restaurante Monzón* (*Plaza San Miguel 3*; 928 70 50 43; www.barmonzon.blogspot.com). Roll up, roll up for *pollo picantón* (spicy chicken), *costillas valsequilleras* (Ribs Valsequillo-stylee), and *callos con garbanzos* (tripe with chickpeas).

Accommodation

Stay in a rural house, the perfect base to explore the area around Valsequillo – a popular destination for hikers. The relatively isolated *El Palmito* (*El Cardón* 10; 928 24 99 80) is accessible by dirt track. More central, but still handy for the *San Miguel Ravine* and adjoining walks, is the historic *Casa Rural El Colmenar* (*Colmenar Bajo* 11; 928 39 01 69).

Nightlife

Get your head down early for a full day's hiking. Not that you have any choice in the matter. Valsequillo aka The City That Always Sleeps is the very antithesis of New York.

Fiestas

There's the mild. As in the *Fiestas del Almendro en Flor* held during the first fortnight of February to celebrate the 2,000+ almond trees in the area flowering. And then there's the wild. As in the *Fiesta de San Miguel*, a month-long party, which culminates in late September with the literally explosive *Suelto del Perro Maldito* (*Release of the Bad Dog*). Here pyrotechnics shine a light on the gruesome costumes sported by revellers.

Attractions

Head out rather than in to discover what Valsequillo truly has to offer. Follow the *Barranco de los Cernícalos* (Kestrel Ravine) from the volcanic crater of *Los Marteles* towards the Telde neighbourhood of *Lomo Magullo*. Flanked by olive trees and willows, there are no shortage of trails to take. The *Tenteniguada* volcanic crater also provides plenty of sights to please sore eyes, including *Roque del Águila* (Eagle Rock).

Europe's Las Vegas

I've lived and worked on Gran Canaria for over six years now. It's like Vegas without the casinos but with all the glitz and glamour. There's so much to see and do here, and not enough days in the week, hours in the day, and so on, to pack everything in.

I've certainly lived the high life. From skydiving over the Maspalomas dunes to bungee jumping in Las Palmas, I've had to develop a head for heights. I've also played for *Club de Rugby de Las Palmas* for the past three years. We've won the double three years in a row in that time, playing in a Canarian league featuring teams from five out of the seven islands.

I've tried my hand at scuba diving, jet skiing, and karting too. You might have seen me salsa dancing or even sambaing in nightclubs. For which I apologize. There's a packed social calendar for the expat to enjoy. Everything from booze cruises to dolphin trips on a daily basis. Look out for the beach and foam parties in the south of the island where I work. You should check out *Playa del Inglés* for these, especially the Kasbah and Irish centres. The Gran Chapparal centre is another great place for expats to meet and greet.

In the south, there's a nice mix of nationalities co-existing side by side. British pubs neighbour German ones which in turn are next to Scandinavian bars. Everybody seems to get on. In fact, it feels like I've met expats from more countries than I've even visited. That's pretty amazing, given how small the island is.

Sure, you can travel around Gran Canaria in one day. But it will take you a lifetime to truly explore what the island has to offer. I'm already playing catch-up.

Lee Anthony Parkes

The jungle without the rumble

SOUTH GRAN CANARIA

Sun? Check. Sea? Check. Sand? Where's it gone? There's something intrinsically fake about the south. As well as its obtrusive *centros comerciales*, much of its sand is imported from the Sahara. There's a reason for this. Serious erosion does go on, with Maspalomas and Taurito frequent victims. There's also the artificial, in more ways than one, beaches of *Amadores* and *Anfi de Mar* which have not been merely topped up but actually created from coral sand hailing from west Africa.

My brother-in-law Sergio's wife Sandra thought a move to the south would have been a gentler introduction to Gran Canaria than the one offered by our relocation to Las Palmas. Not realizing that I knew the south all too well. I'd once been dragged out there by one of my wife's cousins on a stag night which involved visiting venues so behind the times, they were almost post-modern piss takes.

But many foreigners *do* make the south their home. And a little part of me is jealous, especially of their tans. The *panza de burro* even turns me off my beloved north coast and the day I'll join the summer migratory movement of sunseekers seems ever closer.

There's also more diversity than you'd imagine. The giant municipalites of San Bartolomé and Santa Lucía de Tirajana stretch right up, almost to the centre of island. Extending from coast to mountain, from beach to forest, they're keen to develop their rural tourism instead of relying solely on the package tourists.

Fataga

In the present day, the noisiest this pretty village of around 400 inhabitants gets is when a motorcycle rally pulls in for a break. The noisiest Fataga got, however, was when it was still known as *Adfatagad* in the latter stages of the 16th century. Its *barranco (ravine)* of the same name staged many of the bloody battles that took place between the invading Castilians and the native *canarii*.

For drivers, the main road is an easy-on-the-eye stretch of architecture which breaks up the winding GC-60. For gastronomes, the cluster of restaurants on Fataga's main drag offering traditional Canarian cuisine will quell the rumble in their tummies. Meanwhile, wine lovers will delight in the south of the island's sole entry in *Gran Canaria's Wine Route*, www.grancanaria.com/patronato_ turismo/The-Wine-Route.2532.0.html.

Located as it is in the *Valley of a Thousand Palms*, the palm trees won't come as a surprise but the orchards might – featuring apricot, banana, lemon, mango, and orange trees. An oasis from the overpopulated resorts of the south, many would consider Fataga perfect. Not so the mayor of the *San Bartolomé de Tirajana* province, of which Fataga belongs, María del Pino Torres who pledged close to a million Euros in early 2011 for the village to improve its image.

Beaches
As part of San Bartolomé de Tirajana, Fataga is handily placed to enjoy the famous beaches of El Inglés and Maspalomas.

Food
Forego the sangria and instead tuck into the *Desperate-Dan*-sized traditional Canarian food on offer at *Bar Restaurante El Albaricoque* (*Calle Nestor Álamo 4;* 928 79 86 56; www.restaurantealbaricoque.com). The Apricot may be a tourist trap, given its central location. But it's a well-run one at that, and the *mirador* of a terrace has plenty of room with a view.

Accommodation
Mirador Fataga (*Finca La Solana*; 680 11 33 87; www.miradorfataga.es) offers shade to counter the southern sun. This big chill of a farm features three different holiday properties to rent. The *casa prinicipal* (main house) houses travelling parties of between 8-10, the *casa vieja* (old house) sleeps two, and there are two apartments too.

Nightlife
The southern resorts, a hedonist's dream, are a mere half hour away.

Fiestas
The tail end of June and early July sees Fataga unite in professing their love for their favourite fruit, the apricot. The *Fiesta del Albaricoque* kicks off with special events for the kiddies before celebrating a *romería*, a colourful daytime parade. The event culminates in a *verbena*, raucous late-night shindig.

Attractions
Between two and three thousand years BC, Gran Canaria's original inhabitants made their home on the island. In 1341, the Portuguse king Alfonso IV ordered an expedition of the Canaries which discovered an aboriginal town made up of 400 dry-stone houses. *Mundo Aborigen* (*Macizo de Amurga*; 928 17 22 95; www.mundoaborigen.com) which you'll hit just before Fataga, travelling from the south, is a recreation of this settlement. Welcome to their world.

The Ripple Effect

Maspalomas

Maspalomas is much more than the sum of its famous dunes. As well as this nudist zone/protected area, a nature reserve since 1897, there's the iconic *Faro de Maspalomas.* At 68-metres tall, this lighthouse remains many a saviour of ships.

Birdwatchers will marvel at *La Charca*, located due west of the dunes. The Pond provides seasonal sanctuary for migratory birds heading from Europe to Africa. Nature lovers will also be able to spot the curious occurrence of lizards cohabiting with rabbits.

Maspalomas is one of the main resorts on the island. More upmarket than neighbouring Playa del Inglés, it also attracts an older crowd. You won't have to look hard to find accommodation here, ranging from budget apartments to boutique hotels.

Beaches

At 2,710 metres long, Maspalomas is the second longest beach on the island after Las Palmas' Las Canteras. Maspalomas conjures up images of sand but in early 2011 the beach suffered the worst erosion in recorded history. Four-metre-high waves washed sand away. Little wonder the local council tops it up with grains imported from the Sahara.

Food

Location, location, location. Enjoying a prime beachside spot, *El Senador* (*Paseo de Faro S/N;* 928 14 04 96; www.restauranteelsenador.com) also delivers on the food front. Specializing in Mediterreanan cuisine, if you like fish don't hesitate to order *lubina a la sal* (sea bass baked in salt), a dish which has its origins in Galicia. Kids (it's my eldest son Dani's favourite restaurant in the area)/ vegetarians are well catered for too, with an extensive selection of pastas and pizzas.

Accommodation

Perfect your swing at the five-star *Sheraton Salobre Golf Resort & Spa* (*Urbanizacion Salobre Golf;* 928 94 30 00; www.sheratonsalobre.com). Or say hello to their Aloe Spa. Widely considered to be a wonder herb for its healing properties, Aloe vera is native to Gran Canaria. The spa's signature treatment is their Aloe-vera wrap.

For an easier-on-your-wallet alternative, there's always *Apartmentos El Capricho* (*Avenída del Oasis 21;* 928 141 680; www.apartelcapricho.com). Unlike most apartments in the south, this complex doesn't have a swimming pool. You don't need one when the Atlantic Ocean is a mere hop, skip and jump away from the private gardens.

Nightlife
Smarter than its *Holiday World* base would suggest, the inexplicably-monikered *My Song* (*Avenída Touroperador Tui S/N*; 928 73 04 98) comes alive to the sound of salsa every Friday and Saturday night.

Fiestas
So crazy for carnival are the Canarians that after the main one in Las Palmas finishes, many attend the island's second biggest *carnaval* in Maspalamos. Typically held in March, coachloads of *murgas* (satirical clowns) travel down the GC-1 from the capital. If it's at all possible, Maspalamos *Carnaval* is even more gay-friendly than its LP counterpart.

Attractions
You wouldn't expect sunny Maspalomas to be so green but adjoining its golf course is its botantical garden, *Parque Botanico de Maspalomas* (*Avenída Turoperador Neckermann 1*; 664 86 48 67) – 12,000 square metres of plants, ranging from the aesthetically pleasing to those of

medicinal value. You'll come across a very different kind of park 10 minutes' drive away. *Aqualand Maspalomas* (*Carretara Palmitos Park KM* 3; 928 14 05 25; <u>www.aqualand.es/grancanaria</u>) is a water park where the longest and fastest slides should carry a health warning: they're definitely not for the faint-hearted.

Lighting up your life, the Faro de Maspalomas

Meloneras

Even more exclusive than Maspalomas is its relatively new neighbour, Meloneras. With the *cabildo* (council) concerned now with quality as much as quantity of tourists, this resort was designed to bring the wealthier tourist to the island. As a result, there's a greater concentration of four- and five-star hotels in Meloneras than anywhere else on the island. But bargain breaks are available too. The shopping centres are also rather more sensitively designed than the concrete hell of *Playa del Inglés*.

Unlike in Las Palmas, the only homeless you can expect to see on the streets of Meloneras are stray cats. These are no by means unique to the island. I once heard an urban myth that there were so many wild moggies because the Catholic religion meant tomcats couldn't be neutered or female felines spayed.

Beaches

Less than a sixth of the length of Maspalomas, Playa Meloneras is also more conservative than its naughty neighbour. *Zona No Nudista* declares the sign which is also displayed in English (No Nudist Area) and German (*No Nacktbaden*) to prevent any errant swimsuit-shedding. Less smooth than Maspalomas, it's probably best to take to the water with aqua shoes as there are rogue pebbles and rocks.

Food

Predating the resort, *Casa Serafín* (*Centro Comercial Meloneras 114*; 928 14 50 25; www.casaserafin-melonerasplaya.com) claims a 50+-year history. Specializing in one of the most popular imports from the peninsula itself, *paella*, fish and seafood dishes flood its menu. Nearby, if you're as hungry as a stallion for Italian food, say, ahem, *ciao* to *Ciao Ciao Meloneras* (*Centro Comercial Meloneras 128*; 928 14 69 69; www.ciaociaomeloneras.com).

146

Accommodation
The pick of the jaw-to-the-floor hotels gracing this area are *Lopesan* pair *Lopesan Costa Meloneras* (*Mar Mediterraneo 1*; 928 12 81 00) and *Lopesan Villa del Conde* (*Mar Mediterraneo 7*; 928 56 32 00). Check out the spa at the former which includes a womb room designed to simulate being back in the uterus. The latter does a mighty fine impression of the historic centre of Agüimes, with the architects going as far as recreating the town's neoclassical domed church in the hotel's lobby. The friendlier on the family, especially in terms of cost, *Cay Beach Meloneras* (*Calle Mar Baltico S/N;* 928 14 35 97) houses a selection of bungalows and duplexes.

Nightlife
Meloneras is hardly Club 18-30 territory with most of the hotels offering their own in-house entertainment. Staying at the African-themed *Lopesan Baobab* once, I was dismayed to see a talented band of African musicans playing *Don't Cry for Me, Argentina*. They did seem to pep up a bit, as did my spirits, with a spirited rendition of Shakira's *Waka Waka*, mind.

Fiestas
Siesta siesta, no time for fiesta. Meloneras is a place to step back and chill. The exception that proves the rule of Gran Canaria's party-island status.

Attractions
520,000 square metres of fairway, green, rough and bunker, *Lopesan Meloneras Golf* (*GC-500 S/N;* 928

14 53 09) is an 18-hole par-71 course. Designed by the legendary American golf course architect Ron Kirby, who gave Gleneagles a face lift, *LMG*'s a veritable oasis of palm trees and lakes. An on-site golf academy lends a helping hand.

> "There's very little to do on this island if the weather turns bad for tourists (apart from shop, and to be honest I wouldn't want to spend my holiday in a clone commercial centre that you can go to back home)." Katy Bowness bemoans Gran Canaria's practically non-existent cultural tourism.

Playa del Inglés

There are two sides to every coin, so the saying goes. This is especially true of Playa del Inglés. The beach itself is one of the most attractive on the island, but the surrounding *centros comerciales* (shopping centres) are the very definition of ugly.

Frequented by English tourists, it is after all called *The English Beach*, it's even more popular with German visitors. To the extent that many joke it should be rechristened *Playa del Aleman*. In truth, the natives love it as much as foreigners with the August destination of choice for a holiday invariably *El Inglés*.

In actual fact, Playa del Inglés is an all-year-round resort. Many Las Palmas residents own a weekend apartment there. They're the ones making up the traditional Sunday evening *caravana*, which literally translates as caravan by which they mean traffic jam.

Beaches

A mere 10 metres shorter than next-door's Maspalamos, at 2,700 metres *El Inglés* is one of the longest stretches of shoreline on the island. A firm favourite with families, parents nevertheless should keep a close eye on younger children as the waves here are deceptive and can catch you out. Although not one of the main bases on the island, you'll find surfing schools here too.

Food

It's back to Basque for chef Jose Cruz Lopez at *El Portalón,* (*Avenída Tirajana 27*; 928 77 16 22), the in-house restaurant of the four-star *Sol Barbacan* hotel. For Lopez raids his homeland for inspiration with Basque Country cuisine dominating the menu's 85 dishes. Down the road, but equally upmarket, you'll find *Restaurante La Toja* (*Avenída Tirajana 17*; 928 76 11 96; www.latoja-playadelingles.com). Sourcing their produce from the *rias* (estuaries) of Galicia, expect fish and shellfish aplenty.

Accommodation

Where *Lopesan* rules the roost in Meloneras, *Bull Hotels* hit the spot in *Playa del Inglés*. The three-star *Hotel Escorial* (*Avenída de Italia* 6; 928 76 13 50; www.bullhotels.com/escorial) is a four-star establishment in all but name while the similarly understarred *Hotel Eugenia Victoria* (*Avenída de Gran Canaria 26;* 928 76 25 00;

www.bullhotels.com/eugeniavictoria) reimagines the spa as theme park with *Dead Sea*, *Snow Cabin* and *Finnish Sauna* some of the many rooms to explore. Another three-star establishment punching above its weight is *Hotel Parque Tropical* (*Avenída de Italia 1*; 928 77 40 12; www.hotelparquetropical.com). Boasting over a thousand different species of plants, the hotel's beautiful gardens extend to 9,500 square metres and the liberal use of terracotta and wood give the whole complex an authentic Canarian feel.

Nightlife

As day turns to night, the Yumbo Centrum (*Avenída de EEUU 54*; 928 76 41 96; www.cc-yumbo.com) with a liberal sprinkling of fairy dust transforms itself from a run-of-the-mill shopping centre to a throbbing mayhem of drag artistes and glammed-up queens, throwing themselves into the party mood with gay abandon. Elsewhere, rock the Kasbah (Shopping Center) by dancing to the party favourites pumped out at The Garage (www.thegaragegrancanaria.com) or take advantage of the similarly free entry at the more cutting-edge Zig Zags (www.zigzagsgrancanaria.com) in *Shopping Center de Maspalamos*.

Fiestas

A tourist resort dating back to the 1960s, Playa del Inglés has no traditional fiesta calendar. Who's complaining when every night is party night in this raucous resort. It's like a *Groundhog Day* version of Prince's *1999* video.

Attractions

Treat your kids and/or your inner child with a ride on the beach's legendary *banana boat*. Feel the seaspray as you zig zag through the waves. The best part is the dunking which results in this-little-piggy-went-to-market-style squeals of fun.

"At about 10.30pm every night of the year there's a shift change at the Yumbo Centre in Playa del Inglés, Gran Canaria. It's not the staff who are changing over, but the clientele. Before 10.30pm, families browse cheap leather goods and sportswear. German couples with lemon sweaters over their shoulders relax with an after-dinner drink. After 10.30pm – curfew time for families and yellow sweaters – the centre fills with a very different, more hedonistic crowd: higher spending, better haircuts. It may be the archetypal package-tour resort, but Playa del Inglés/Maspalomas is also the biggest gay resort in Europe. And the Yumbo Centre is its epicentre." *The Guardian's* Neville Walker gets to grips with Gran Canaria's gay scene.

San Agustín

My wife Cristina, as she never tires of telling me, used to holiday in San Agustín every summer. We spent the first nights of our honeymoon in the resort's *Dunas Don Gregory* hotel. Yet one near-tragic episode on San Agustín's *Playa Las Burras* changed everything.

We'd headed down south for a spot of sun and had already contacted some in-laws who live in *El Tablero* to see if they wanted to join us on their favourite beach.

"No, it's too windy," they tell us.

Now Gran Canaria is one of the windiest places I've ever experienced so we think nothing of it and continue to *Playa Las Burras*. We're able to picnic despite the gusts from above. It isn't until I lay my head down to enjoy a *siesta* that the weather goes wild.

I awake to see parasols swirling in the air above me. After rubbing my eyes in disbelief, I notice that my eldest son Dani is caught between shielding himself from the mini-tornado and running to the safety of his brother and mother. I move quickly and softly rugby-tackle him, so that I'm effectively shielding him from any blows. Which results in concussion and a motorbike ride to the nearest casualty. Suffice to add but I haven't set foot on *Las Burras* since.

Quieter than Playa del Inglés, not so pretensious as Maspalomas, San Agustín nevertheless remains a popular resort. Split into three sections by dividing rocks, the beach is a 670-metre stretch of dark sand. With fewer waves than other southern beaches, it's a haven for scuba divers and snorkellers.

Beaches

Take your chances at *Las Burras* which inexplicably survives as a popular choice for families. Despite the fact that a fellow expat told me he didn't understand its kiddy-friendly status because of the dangerous local undercurrents. Alternatively, there's the main beach.

Food

Visit the house that Jacques (Truyol) built, *Restaurant Anno Domini* (*Centro Comercial San Agustín 82;* 928 76 29 15; www.restaurantannodomini.com). Although operating from a rather tired-looking shopping centre, the French chef never flags with his renditions of Gallic classics. Along with interpretations of popular Canarian and Italian dishes.

Accommodation

You'll discover two of Gran Canaria's best spa hotels in San Agustín. The four-star *Gloria Palace Thalasso & Hotel* (*Calle Las Margaritas S/N*; 928 12 85 00) opened the first thalassotherapy centre on the island, *Talasoterapia Canarias*, back in 1998. Closer to the beach, you'll come across the five-star *Melía Tamarindos* (*Calle Retama 3*, 928 77 40 90; www.melia-tamarindos.com) where you'll find it difficult to leave the comforts on offer at this vast complex.

Nightlife

Drunk and disorderly's not really an option in San Agustín. For those sort of shenanigans, shameless Playa del Inglés next door is the place. Though, you can demonstrate your poker face at the Hotel Melía Temarindos' casino (*Calle Retama 3*; 928 76 27 24; www.casinotamarindos.es) which is open to non-guests.

Fiestas

As befits its resort status, San Agustín doesn't celebrate any local fiestas.

Attractions

Originally the film set for legendary western *A Fistful of Dollars*, *Sioux City* (*Barranco del Águila S/N*; 928 76 25 73; www.siouxcity.es) now boasts the tagline "Where the West is Fun". Explore a lovingly-recreated period of American history, replete with bank, sheriff's office, and saloon. Best for kids during the day, adult-orientated shows light up the place at night.

"An Eden Project style giant biosphere in one of the empty valleys behind Bahia Feliz and San Agustín might be just what is needed. Picture a huge greenhouse with all the world's major ecosystems inside. Visitors would be able to travel through a rainforest canopy along raised walkways and see crocodiles and Amazon animals from boardwalks over a swamp. The climate on the island is ideally suited to the project and the idea is bang on trend with eco-awareness growing across Europe. Six million people, many foreign tourists, visited the original Eden Project in Cornwall in its first four years!" Alex Bramwell on Gran Canaria's need for something new, albeit something borrowed.

San Bartolomé de Tirajana

The annual tourism figures for *Maspalomas*, *Playa del Inglés*, and *San Agustín* make the area to which they all belong the most visited of all of Spain. Paying homage to this, the local council, *Illustre Ayuntamiento de la Villa de San Bartolomé de Tirajana* registered the following domain for their official website: www.maspalomas.com. Yet beyond the dunes there's much to explore.

The largest municipality on the island by far, *San Bartolomé de Tirajana* nearly makes up a third of Gran Canaria. Located in the south-east of the island, *SBDT*'s permanent population has virtually doubled since the 1990s and now numbers in excess of 45,000. As well as tourism, agriculture and business are the other key industries.

It's a land of contrasts too. The relatively built-up San Fernando area's a world away from rural paradise Fataga. But all that separates the two is a 16km-ish stretch road.

Beaches

Away from the main resorts, we initially couldn't work out what all the fuss was about *Bahia Feliz* (Happy Bay). Jostling for space on a miniscule rocky beach, our smiles came out along with the tide which revealed a sandy beach straight out of a *Bounty* ad. One place that's never short of sand is *Montaña de Arena* (Sand Mountain). Located in the *Bahia de Santa Agueda* collection of out-of-the-way beaches, it's a 10-minute walk from car park to shore.

Food

The future's orange if the décor at *Bamira* (*Calle Los Pinos 11*; 928 76 66 66; www.bamira.com) is anything to go by. German owners Anna and Herbert Eder, architects of Gran Canaria's introduction to fusion cookery, or "adventure cuisine" as they call it, combine ingredients and recipes sourced from near and afar in the decidedly non-starry setting of *Playa de Águila*. A perfect example's their marriage of the Central European with the Canarian in their *Octopus and Pork Belly goulash*.

Accommodation

Hotel Rural Las Tirajanas (*Calle Oficial Mayor José Rubio S/N;* 928 12 30 00; www.hotel-lastirajanas.com) wouldn't look out of place in the Alps. Flanked by pines and nestling between mountains, the only giveaway that you're not in an Alpine setting are the palm trees. Playa del Ingles, a mere 40 minutes away, it's not.

Nightlife
Playa del Inglés dominates the nocturnal scene in *SBDT*. Elsewhere, keep your eyes peeled for tumbleweeds. And not only at *Sioux City*.

Fiestas
Tunte aka *San Bartolomé de Tirajana*, the town not the municipality, forms the centre of *Fiestas en honor a San Bartolomé* in August. One way the locals pay tribute is to feast on a giant *sancocho canario* (sea-bass stew) in the town's main square. Easter with its obvious religious connotations brings the *Fiestas del Niño Dios* to Ayagaures. The final day sees a raffle where the lucky winners can walk off with a live pig or even kid, as in goat.

Attractions
Make like a F1 driver at the *Gran Karting Club* (*Carretera General del Sur KM 46*; 928 15 71 90; www.grankarting. com). Located 10 minutes north of *Playa del Ingles*, you can't miss it as it's well signposted and indeed visible off the GC1. Featuring four tracks for age groups ranging from under 5s up to adults, feel the wind in your hair as you reach speeds of up to 80kph.

"Whether your idea of a good holiday is visiting the country vineyards and sampling homemade wine, horse riding and parascending, dancing the night away in the discos or just relaxing and enjoying the many beaches and sights, Gran Canaria has something for everyone." The Cunning Canary aka Victoria Smith sums up the island's assets.

Santa Lucía de Tirajana

From mountain high to valley low, there's plenty to see in this south-east municipality. Agriculture employs the most in this farming area. You'll first hit Saint Lucy travelling southwards on the GC-1 from Las Palmas, roughly 20 minutes into your journey.

The historic meets the modern in *SLDT*. From the traditional centre of the municipality, Santa Lucía, to the uber-contemporary Vecindario, you'll be able to travel back and forwards in time. From the pre-Spanish fortress of *Fortelaza de Ansite* to *Centros Comerciales Avenida de Canarias, Atlantico, and La Ciel* – the trio of shopping centres which dominate the Vecindario skyline.

Yet if its architecture isn't traditional, you can still glimpse history in Vecindario. The municipality's *Handcraft Centre* is located in its largest town. Here, you can see basketwork, cutlery and pottery being made, right before your very eyes.

Beaches

More rural than coastal, Santa Lucía de Tirajana can only count one beach as its own. At 1,280 metres long, *Pozo Izquierdo*'s a sports beach. With winds reaching speeds of up to 60kph, it's established itself as the premier windsurfing centre on the island.

Food

The fruits of the region's olive trees are put to good use, as bar snack of choice in Santa Lucía de Tirajana's hostelries. The local *Ansite* wines are popular as is a rather more mysterious beverage known as *Mejunje de Ventura*, a concoction of white rum, honey, brown sugar, lemon, lemongrass, cinnamon, and coffee. Bag a terrace table at the appropriately-named *El Viento*, The Wind (*Avenída Punta Tenefé 2*; 928 12 10 11), to watch the windsurfers in action.

Accommodation

Never miss a flight by staying at the four-star *Elba Vecindario Aeropuerto* (*Avenída Atlántico* 353; 928 72 43 00; www.hoteleselba.com). 10 minutes from the airport, it's also surprisingly a good base to explore the whole of the island. Planning on some serious shopping? The Vecindario shopping centre of the same name houses the two-star *Hotel Avenida de Canarias* (*Avenida Canarias* 264; 928 75 47 76; www.hotelavenidadecanarias.com), so carrying those bags is less of a burden. Lovers of the great outdoors will find more appropriate accommodation at *Casa Rural Cercado de Don Paco* (*Calle Pago de Ingenio S/N;* 928 43 18 68). A converted barn and tool shed, it lies footsteps away from local hiking routes.

Nightlife

My wife Cristina shocked me when she told me she used to go nightclubbing in shopping centres in her youth. This is a practice I've discovered since moving here that still goes on. And in Shopping Central Vecindario, the *Centro Comerciales* are your best option if you find yourself in carousing mode.

Fiestas

December is party time in Santa Lucía. On the 13th December, they celebrate *El Día de Santa Lucía*, a bonkers hybrid of Catholicism, Lutherism, and Paganism. In the capital of the municipality, a Canarian girl and a Swedish girl play the part of Lucy, the patron saint of sight, and lead a procession which ends up at the village church culminating in a fertility ritual and mass.

The following Sunday marks *El Día del Trabajador*, the Day of the Labourer. In honour of the *Virgen del Rosario*, villagers decked out in traditional garb follow a procession of carts drawn by cattle or tractors. Each cart carries a product associated with the region, whether it be gofio, sardines, or even a pumpkin full of *Mejunje de Ventura*, which is distributed freely to party-goers.

Attractions

In 1483, *Bentejuí*, the last of the *guanarteme* (aboriginal kings) and his men threw themselves off the *Fortelaza de Ansite* aka *Fortelaza Grande* rather than surrender and convert to Christianity. Discover further details about this at the more centrally-located *Museo Castillo de la*

Fortaleza (*Calle Tomás Arroya Cardosa S/N*; 928 79 80 07), an archaeological museum that's an unbeatable treat in the heart of Santa Lucía village.

Atlantic Fantastic

When I first came to Gran Canaria I admit I wasn't impressed. It's hardly the prettiest island. In fact, it's very arid and rocky. Apart from the odd glimpse of the ocean, there's not much to look at travelling from the airport to Puerto Rico. I wasn't even sure if I wanted to live here.

But then I grew to love the beautiful Atlantic views around every bend when driving to the shops and after a day in the breathtaking Grand-Canyon-esque mountains, I was almost persuaded. The sun would shine almost all the time, but still I wasn't entirely convinced I could live here permanently.

Well, I've been here for almost four years now so what made up my mind? We found a boat. It wasn't a big boat and it wasn't a pretty boat, but soon it was our boat. We cleaned this very neglected boat and my partner Trevor who happens to be a very good mechanic fixed the engine. Then we updated the upholstery. Finally, we had a seaworthy boat.

Suddenly we were talking to all sorts of people down the harbour. I was introduced to fishing for the first time. Yes, I miss being in *B&Q* on a Sunday but not for long because most Sundays we are fishing, or snorkelling, or just bobbing about on the water, and thinking how lucky we are.

There's a season for marlin and people come from all over the world to catch this elusive yet large swordfish. They come to fish but sometimes I think they come to talk. They'll tell you about their first-ever marlin, their biggest marlin, or the trickiest marlin.

You can spend hours and hours and hours sitting on a boat trolling. There's the first hour or two of expectation, a few hours of boredom (if you're lucky), then an exhausting half hour or more of such an euphoria-packed adrenalin rush that makes all the waiting worth while. Most marlin caught have a mug shot taken before being set free.

For me, it's not so much the fishing; it's the whole fishing community you become a part of. We always stop for a drink in the harbour just to chill and catch up on who caught what, where and how. Of course, there's always a fisherman's tale.

Jacqui Jones

WEST GRAN CANARIA

Red Sky at Night, Ain't Tenerife Bright

A bugger to get to because of its winding approach roads (the GC-2 goes no further than Agaete although workman are currently drilling through the mountains to link the nearby El Risco with La Aldea de San Nicolás via a tunnel): the west of the island's just as difficult to leave. And not only because of its winding departure roads, but also due to the fact it's one of the best places on the island to live. To the extent, that I'm now seriously contemplating an escape from Las Palmas to the west rather than my beloved north coast because of the dreaded *panza de burro*, donkey's belly, the big black cloud that engulfs the north of the island in summer.

The GC-200 that takes you from Agaete on to La Aldea de San Nicolás usually causes my children to return the food from whence it entered their body. In blogger Alex Bramwell's opinion, though it "must be one of Europe's top drives." "If you like your motoring", he continues "it's worth renting a good car for the day to experience the curves and switch-backs."

But the GC-200 is under serious threat because of its inaccessibility. As the ever-informative Bramwell reveals: "The road won't be around for ever. Plans are afoot for a faster inland route and eventually the original road will be allowed to drop into the sea. Apparently its potential as a tourist route isn't high enough to justify the costs of clearing after the rains."

Another way of reaching La Aldea is from the south, travelling through Mogán. My brother-in-law Jorge offered to take our son, Alex, this way to see if this would solve his travel sickness. All was fine, until the very last bend which prompted an out-of-body experience with ectoplasm to boot.

Agaete

So cherished is the pretty town of Agaete that locals have a saying: "See Agaete and leave." They are worried of any unwanted change. Yet their fears have been unfounded, even the new developments have been incorporated sensitively with the whitewashed exteriors blending in with the traditional properties.

However, we nearly took the locals at their word. Showing my relatives another side of the island prior to our wedding we 'enjoyed' a lunch at a restaurant in Agaete's Port of Snow, *Puerto de las Nieves*. Before succumbing to a particularly explosive form of food poisoning.

But as the memory subsided, we did return. Agaete perfectly illustrates the difference between people born on the island and those who have come to live here from overseas. A mere 30km from the capital, locals consider a commute to Las Palmas a commute too far. Not so Jackie, a native English teacher I used to work with, and her publisher husband Richard who have made Agaete very much their home.

Beaches

The beaches of *Puerto de las Nieves*, *Del Muelle* and *Las Nieves* are nothing to write home about, either being too pebbly or too rocky. Yet travel out of town a little and you'll be rewarded. *El Risco* looks like the very ends of the Earth, unless you travel there on a bank holiday when it's besieged by motor caravans. The similarly out-of-the-way *Guayedra*, accessible only after descending the *barranco* (ravine) of the same name, wields a magnetic appeal over nudists.

Food

I genuinely can't recall the name of the offending restaurant which struck my family and I down pre-wedding. Nevertheless, the seafront eateries in *Puerto de las Nieves* are much of a muchness, none really stands out.

Unlike the nearby *La Palmita* (*Carretara Puerto de Las Nieves S/N*; 928 89 87 04) whose acclaimed *cocina de playa* (beach cuisine) includes the freshest gold sea-bream *(sama)*, horse mackerel (*jurel*), and sea bass *(corvina)*.

Accommodation

There are more hidden extras than on a DVD boxset but you're still guaranteed a reassuringly luxurious stay at the four-star *Roca Negra* (*Avenida Alfredo Kraus* 42; 928 89 80 09; www.hotelrocanegragrancanaria.com). Equally upmarket but in a more central situation, there's *Hotel Puerto de las Nieves* (*Avenida Alcade José de Armas S/N;* 928 88 62 56; www.hotelpuertodelasnieves.es), also a four-star. The nearby verdant *Valle de Agaete*, Agaete Valley, boasts the charm offensive otherwise known as *Finca Las Longueras* (*Carretara Antigua de Agaete SN*; 928 89 81 45; www.laslongueras.com). This rural hotel, a converted mansion, lies in the grounds of a plantation producing avocados, bananas, oranges, and papayas.

Nightlife

The cool as opposed to chilly evenings invite a nocturnal *paseo* (stroll). You're not going to find any scene but you'll be able to indulge in one of the island's favourite sports: people watching. Dare to stare.

Fiestas

My personal favourite party on Gran Canaria is the *Fiesta de la Bajada de la Rama*. Held in early August, it starts with branches being snapped off the pine trees of the *Pinar de Tamadaba* forest, located at over 900 metres altitude. A raucous procession, accompanied by the Agaete Municipal Band, descends to the seafront. At each house the crowd stop and cry for "*aguita, aguita* (water, water)" and then cheer loudly as it's poured over their heads. Upon reaching the port, revellers thrash the branches in the sea, mimicking a pre-Christian ritual to ensure adequate rain falls in order to grow next season's crops.

Attractions

Buy from the world's most northerly and Europe's only coffee plantations at the *AGROAGAETE* shop in the town's *Plaza Tomás Morales*. The agreeable temperature, abundant water and volcanic soil make the valley bordering the town a fertile breeding ground for coffee beans. In 1788 the Spanish king Carlos III issued a decree permitting the importation of the first coffee plants to this island. Produced using the natural method of sun-drying the bean without removing the pulp, the result is a coffee with fruity undertones and a hint of chocolate.

"One of the most interesting things to note about the early years of surfing in Arguineguín was the surfer settlements. The campsite next to the football stadium was once forested and had become home to hippies and surfers alike. Surfers from all around the world (Hawaii, California, England and Australia) lived here – as well as in settlements in Tauro and Aldea. They fished, surfed the waves and enjoyed the relaxed lifestyle and fantastic Arguineguin sunsets… so extensive was the surf community here, guys were even building surfboards from their forest hippy commune!" *Surf Canaries'* Daniel Alcock on the days before a surf board became the middle-classes' favourite plaything.

Arguineguín

We first discovered Arguineguín by accident. In my continued quest to visit all the beaches on the island, I'd pressganged Alex and Dani to accompany me to *El Pirata*, spinning the line that we might see *Jack Sparrow* there. Alighting at San Agustín, I approach a taxi driver (always a mistake) and ask him how to get there. Feigning confusion, he replies: "*¿El Pirata, El Pirata? No, no, no, Las Burras.*"

Not wishing to return to a scene of previous misfortune, we walk off to ask somebody else before the taxi driver shouts out, "*¿El Pirata, El Pirata? Sí, sí, sí"* and motions for us to jump in. 15 minutes/ €20 Euros later he drops us off at what I later discover to be Patalavaca, pointing us absent-mindedly in the direction of what will turn out to be Arguineguín.

Stopping off for a break at the 'natural' swimming pool of *Playa La Lajilla*, we're impressed by a red-bodied blonde-headed boy's full bucket of fish, seeing as he's using just a line and bread. After lunching in the town, having given up on *El Pirata*, we relax on Arguineguín's main beach before returning home. By bus.

Beaches

The 100 metres of dark sand which make up Arguineguín's shoreline is also known as *Playa de las Marañuelas*. Not a looker by any stretch of the imagination, it's still popular with local families. Including the many Scandinavians who have made Arguineguín their home.

Food

Asia on a plate, Arguineguín's a hotspot for lovers of sweet and sour cuisine. Well worth navigating Arguineguín's back streets is the tucked-away *Fusion Restaurant & Lounge Bar* (*Calle Alonso Quesada 13;* 928 18 56 62; www.fusionrestaurantandloungebar.com), purveyors of south-east Asian dishes including *Beef Redang,* a slow-cooked spicy Indonesian beef curry, and the classic *Pad Thai*. Elsewhere, *Restaurante Chino Lun* (*Carretara General del Sur 23;* 928 185066; www.restaurantechinolun. es) has built a solid, unfussy reputation amongst locals and tourists alike – they also deliver as far afield as *Anfi del Mar* and *Tauro*.

Accommodation

For a superior three-star holiday experience, look no further than H*otel Dorado Beach* (*Avenida de los Canarios* 1; 928 15 07 80; www.bullhotels.com/doradobeach). Child-friendly to the extent the free basement spa's open to kids at certain times, the top-floor solarium with jacuzzi offers an ocean view along with the sun and bubbles. The pool area providing direct access to the beach of *La Lajilla* features a swimming pool which is heated in winter to guarantee all-year-round usability.

Nightlife

The local bars are lively 365 days a year mainly because Arguineguín is as much as place to live as a place to holiday. Failing that, the hotels put on the usual shows. Of varying quality.

Fiestas

July brings the *Fiestas del Carmen* to Arguineguín. The *chiringuitos* (temporary food shacks) offer an introductory selection of local foods and beverages. Check out the beauty conquest otherwise known as the *Gala de Elección de la Reina de las Fiestas*.

Attractions

Take the plunge at *Dive Academy* (*Calle La Lajilla S/N*; 928 73 61 96; www.diveacademy-grancanaria.com) which uses its own pool to teach budding ocean explorers. Those already qualified can enjoy daily boat trips to explore the many reefs and wrecks the island has to offer, with the chance to see angel sharks, octopus and turtles, amongst countless other wonders of the deep.

La Aldea de San Nicolás

O Little Town of Aldea de San Nicolás

If it's New Year, it must be La Aldea de San Nicolás which once upon a time was known as an island within an island because of it's isolation from the rest of Gran Canaria. Up until more recently than you imagine, locals would travel by boat to Tenerife to stock up on provisions rather than the more-distant Las Palmas. My mother in law Ceci is a member of the Angulo family who own the *SunTom* group. Growing tomatoes on their farms, they export them to greengrocers and supermarkets in England, France, Germany, and Scandinavia.

On the main farm, she has a property – a sizeable property which shrinks before your very eyes however as her numerous grandchildren arrive (19 at the last count) with their parents in tow. Brother-in-law Victor stuffs the old wood stove with meat, having already liberally applied his special marinade. After a long drawn-out dinner on the 31st, we bring in the New Year with *las uvas*. Spanish tradition dictates that for each midnight chime you must eat a grape.

In *La Aldea de San Nicolás*, there's surf as in the totally tropical beach of Güigüi and turf as in the agricultural area where the farms are and the *Parque Rural del Roque Nublo*, the largest protected area on the island. Check out the avenue of palm trees fashioned to look like pineapples on the road which links the provincial capital, *La Aldea de San Nicolas* to its port, *Puerto de la Aldea*. While *San Nicolás'* main church is as young as me (we were both born in 1972), the *Museo Vivo* (*Calle Piedra La Mesa S/N*; 928 89 24 25) offers a snapshot of an older Aldea with an overview of its commercial, educational, and farming history.

Beaches

Puerto de la Aldea's the port of *La Aldea de San Nicolas*, the provincial capital. The beach here's nothing to get excited about and actually it's more fun to jump into the sea from the harbour, considerably safer than tombstoning I guarantee. More special is the sub-*Treasure Island* secret cove accessed by the rockpools to the right of the port.

And then there's the isolated beach of *Güigüi*, also known as *Go-Guy* (with the former pronunciation first emerging from a confused tourist's mouth) – a place so out of the way it's accessible only by boat, or by foot. If you travel from Tasartico's Cañada de Aguasabinas, the trek will take you from 90 minutes to two and a half hours; whereas from La Aldea's El Tarahalillo it's a more time-consuming journey, between four and six hours.

Güigüi is actually two beaches rather than one. *Güi Güi Grande* is rocky and rubbish-strewn. Its neighbour, *Güi Güi Chico*, looks like something out of a *Lilt* commercial. You can only safely cross over between the two when the tide is low but make like the locals – lifting your rucksack high above your head to wade on through.

Food

They do things differently in the wild west of Gran Canaria with their own take on a classic Canarian dish, *Ropa Vieja de Pulpo* (© *Restaurante La Oliva, Playa de Tasarte*). Here octopus replaces chicken as one of this recipe's principal ingredients. Elsewhere, the restaurants aren't as adventurous, offering solid rather than spectacular renditions of classic Canarian dishes.

You get the sense that eateries are popular because of the relative lack of alternatives. *Restaurante La Gañanía* (*Calle El Albercón 4*; 928 89 01 62; www.laganania.galeon.com) is no exception, although sipping on the freshest fruit juice on the island in the immaculately-preserved cactus garden is one of life's simple pleasures. As is dining outdoors at turn-up-and-ask-for-a-table *Bar Avenida* (*Calle Vardero 6)* where if a *cubata* (rum and Coke) doesn't refresh you, the inevitable gusts of wind will.

Accommodation

Canarians don't really do camping. The pick of the few sites on the island, though, can be found close to *Tasartico's* beach. At *Camping Villamar* (*Barranco de Tasartico;* 928 89 02 45) offering cabins and caravans alongside pitchable-tent space, they keep campers happy with a bar, minimarket, and pool.

For many years, *La Aldea de San Nicolás* was a one-hotel town. The homely one-star *Hotel Cascajos* (*Calle Los Cascajos* 9; 982 89 11 65; www.hotelcascajos.com) now has some competition in the flash form of the three-star *Hotel La Aldea Suites* (*Calle Transversal Federico Rodríguez S/N;* 928 89 10 35; www.laaldeasuites.com). While the former rooms don't come equipped with air conditioning, the suites housed in the latter feature state-of-the-art design.

Nightlife

Less bling than its name suggests, *Disco Cristal* (*Calle Federico Rodriguez S/N*; 654 39 79 03) is the region's only nightclub along with *Disco Avenida*. Bear in mind these clubs open from midnight to five in the morning on Friday and Saturday evenings only. Not that this pair of venues ever get as busy as their counterparts in the southern resorts.

Fiestas

Easily the highlight of *LADSN's* uncluttered social calendar is the *Fiesta del Charco* on the 11th September, with 20,000 locals descending on La Aldea in the oldest party on the island. Predating the Spanish Conquest, merry revellers clad in T-shirts (to appease the Church) try to catch the native *lisa* fish in a lagoon, using just their bare hands.

Attractions

Taking full advantage of its arid surroundings, *Cactualdea* (*Carretera del Hoyo S/N*; 928 89 12 28) is a cacti garden worth going out of the way to see. Boasting in excess of 1,200 different species, you're free to pay to enter this display from 10am to 6pm every day of the week. This garden also has an on-site restaurant.

Mogán

Mogán, the region, is one of the areas where there's a whole lot of development going on with the municipality challenging *San Bartolome de Tirajana* as the tourist destination of choice on Gran Canaria. Mogán, the village, one suspects hasn't changed in centuries yet along decades. *Viva la diferencia.*

The second largest municipality on the island in terms of area, its population doesn't even number 20,000 – visitors excluded. As well as beach bums, posteriors attached to more active torsos can be seen walking along many of the well-maintained paths in *Mogán's* interior. For holiday snaps free of an ice cream and/or beach ball, check out the *charcos azules* (blue pools) you'll find on a trek in the *Barranco de Veneguera* area.

Other popular hiking routes take in the *Presa de Soria*, the island's largest reservoir. Nearby water cascades in the streams and rivers of *La Inagua* which is also home to a substantial pine forest. And if you're driving on the island after heavy rain, waterfalls appear on the road linking Mogán to *Pico de las Nieves*.

Beaches

Whilst the beaches of the resorts including P*uertos Mogan* and *Rico* draw the families who holiday together, the rustic trio of *El Medio Almud, Los Frailes*, and *Tiritaña* are clothing-optional hangouts (literally). *Veneguera*'s a rural beach saved as developers wanted to create a new *Playa del Ingles* here before opposition from locals, so it remains accessible only by dirt track.

Food

Restaurante Grill Acaymo (*Calle El Tostador 14;* 928 56 92 63; www.restauranteacaymomogan.com) is as Canarian as they come. From the Canary-yellow interior to the non-English-speaking staff, you won't forget your meal here in a hurry. In Patalavaca, food ranges from the sublime at the critically-acclaimed *Restaurante La Aquarela* (*Barranco de la Verga* 5; 928 73 58 91; www.restaurantelaaquarela. com) to the ridiculous at local heroes *Pizzeria Magico*

(*Carretera General del Sur S/N;* 928 56 12 37), an eatery championed by Yolanda, the wife of my *cuñado*/brother-in-law Jorge, who insists I mention their pizza topped with bananas and curry.

Accommodation

The four-star *Hotel Paradise Costa Taurito* (*Calle Alcazaba* 1; 928 56 59 19) assures a relaxing break. A mere 200 metres from Taurito's sandy beach, if you can drag yourself away from *Lago Oasis*, at 1,350 square metres Gran Canaria's largest saltwater pool, that is. Luxury for those on a budget, the three-star *Hotel Puerto de Mogán* (*Urbanización Puerto de Mogan S/N*; 928 56 50 66; www.hotelpuertodemogan.com) enjoys an enviable position in the port which shares its name. With views over the harbour and Atlantic, the on-site diving centre is yet another plus.

Nightlife

Harleys Dancing (www.harleys-dancing.com)? Dirty dancing more like. A 1980s-style throwback of a club, this Puerto Rico venue unsurprisingly finds favour with hen parties.

Fiestas

Tony, Tony, Tony. San Antonio dominates the traditional party scene in Mogán. June 13th, the feast day of San Antonio de Padua, the patron saint of the municipality, brings the *Fiestas de San Antonio El Chico*. First, a parade sees Puerto de Mogán locals carrying fruit and home-made goods as offerings to the saint before the procession concludes with a display of the statue of the saint while all join in by singing the *Canto de los Pajaritos*. Later, on the first Sunday of August, the denizens of Puerto de Mogán participate in the *Fiestas de San Antonio El Grande*, a communal response to a plague of locusts destroying the municipality's crops.

Attractions

Las Palmas' charmingly-named *Calle de Molino de Viento (Windmill Street)* is a notorious red-light district in the *Arenales* district of town. This mini Amsterdam is a strip of rip-off bars and whorehouses. Mogán's *Molino de Viento*, meanwhile, a bucolic hamlet no less boasts a lovingly-restored windmill that looks like something from *Don Quixote's* times.

Puerto de Mogán

Cesar Manrique would certainly approve of the low-rise low-level buzz of *Puerto de Mogán*. Manrique was a famous artist based in Lanzarote. An activist rather than recluse, CM successfully pressganged the Lanzarote authorities into ensuring new developments were built no taller than two-storeys high.

Over in Gran Canaria, capital Las Palmas wants to recreate the big-city feel of other more famous metropolises, with the flash new apartments on *Calle Luís Doreste Silva* marketed as *La Gran Manzana* (The Big Apple) by eyes-on-the-prize property developers. *Puerto de Mog*án is the very antithesis of that with a less-is-more approach.

The intricate network of canals linking the harbour to the bijou marina have even earned the resort a "Little Venice" sobriquet.

Another Manrique stipulation was that residential property, be it old or new, should be whitewashed and draped in *bougainvillea*, the ornamental clambering plant typically flowering into a shock of pink. True to form, *PDM's* properties are as white as freshly-polished teeth and burgeoning with *bougainvillea*. How very Lanzarote.

Beaches

Sunlight bounces off the golden sand at *Playa Mogán*. At 190 metres long, this is a chic petite beach. An obvious favourite with tourists, you could play *Spot the Local* with little joy.

Food

Carbohydrate up at *La Lonja* (*Puerto de Mogán* 116; 928 56 54 76; www.lalonjamogan.com) where generous portions of both rice and potato, along with other vegetables in season, accompany the many fish dishes. Whether you like your *atún*/tuna *a la plancha*/grilled or *encebellado*/ combined with onion in a soup, the kitchen cooks your selection of the latest catches at your discretion. Owned by the same people, *Restaurante Varadero* (*Explanada del Castillete* 5; 928 56 56 10) nevertheless is an altogether different proposition to its partner restaurant. For one thing, it boasts a swimming pool; for another, there's more a focus on Canarian recipes over the internationalism of *La Lonja*.

Accommodation

In China, the collective sweet tooth of the population has created the need for restaurants offering just desserts. The classy *Los Guayres*, in-house restaurant of the four-star *Hotel Cordial Mogán Playa* (*Avenida de los Marreros 2*; 928 72 41 00) is similarly pudding-obsessed with a special separate room for you to enjoy your afters. Special mention must also go out to the on-site *Spa Inagua* which offers seaweed wraps amongst other treatments on its extensive menu. All in all, the *Cordial Mogán* shows the acceptable face of tourism on the island.

Nightlife

There's no curfew, but there might as well be. In a bid to keep *Puerto de Mogán* neat and petite, the resort doesn't do clubs. Try Puerto Rico instead where dancing around your handbag remains the craze that won't die out.

Fiestas

Roam around the *romería* which hits Puerto de Mogan in June. Traditionally, a *romería*'s a pilgrimage. Essentially, it's an excuse for a street party with locals donning traditional costumes and dancing like it's 1599.

Attractions

Take a trip to Davy Jones' Locker with a voyage on *Puerto de Mogán's* distinctive *Yellow Submarine* (*Atlántida Submarine, Local 389*; 928 56 51 08; www. atlantidasubmarine.com). Whilst under the sea, you'll be able to see a shipwreck and schools, nay universities, of fish. Alternatively, keep your head above water on a two-hour glass-bottomed-boat trip to Arguineguín.

Puerto Rico

The official languages of Puerto Rico, the country, are Spanish and English. It feels much the same in Puerto Rico, the resort. Easily the most touristy place in *Mogán*, the use of sign language remains the exclusive preserve of the deaf here.

In the '60s, Puerto Rico, as we know it now, didn't exist. The entire resort's an artifice. Workmen started blasting into the mountain in 1968 with construction beginning a year later.

As well as tourists, there's a healthy expat community in Puerto Rico. *RTN Canarias* once sent me down there to interview husband-and-wife team, Dr David and nurse Mary, at their *British Medical Clinic*. They relocated from the north of the island because of the greater demand for English-speaking healthcare in the south-west.

Beaches
In line with its man-made origins, the sand on Puerto Rico's beach comes from the Sahara. The quarter-kilometre stretch of shoreline snakes round a postcard-pretty horseshoe-shaped bay. Arguably the sunniest spot on the island, tan-topping has never seemed so appropriate.

Food

Best book ahead for a table at the popular *Caballito de Mar* (*Calle de los Olimpicos Doreste y Molina* 46; 928 72 55 62). Despite its name, the Seahorse's menu is international in focus rather than specializing in local fish dishes. For the traditionalist at heart, the dinner and dance at *Bahia Playa* (*Avenida Juan Díaz Rodriguez* 8; 928 56 01 56; www.bahiaplaya.es) provides the perfect excuse to polish and shine those dancing shoes.

Accommodation

Disconnect at the entirely relaxing *Marina Suites* (*Calle Juan Díaz Rodriguez* 10; 928 15 30 15; www. marinasuitesgrancanaria.com). Take pleasure at your leisure at a hotel which appears to be standing still, even the lifts are reported as slower than elsewhere. Whilst the *Marina Suites Kids Pool* will keep your children entertained, the *Infinity Pool* has to be seen to be believed, seemingly stretching into the adjoining Atlantic Ocean.

Nightlife

Dicey Reillys (*CC Puerto Rico*; www.diceyreillys.com) is where the craic's at. A little piece of the Emerald Isle transplanted to Puerto Rico, it's one of the best places to spend St Patrick's Night on the island. Especially after Sheehans in Las Palmas was sold by its original owners.

Fiestas

Move along now. Nothing to see here. Puerto Rico is simply too new to have any tradition of old-school Canarian partying.

Attractions

There be dolphins in Puerto Rico. *Animal Encounters* (666 12 47 76; www.animalencounters.info) offer regular excursions departing from the pier at Puerto Rico for you to catch a glance at these amazing mammals. The cost of the ticket includes paella and drinks.

Plenty to Carp About

I got the call whilst I was out on the boat in the 'lake', baiting up.

"Hi, it's Scott Maslen here from EastEnders".

After the initial shock, we arranged some dates for Scott to come over and fish with us. Gran Canaria is not your usual carp-fishing holiday destination but Scott had heard from friends how great it was and approached us at Canary Island Carp Fishing Tours to find out more.

Scott travelled over with his friend, the ex-UK-carp-record-holder, Simon Bater. After meeting them at the airport, we drove up the mountains to 'Lake' *Chira* (it's actually a reservoir) where they spent the duration of their stay. The week went splendidly with glorious sunshine and temperatures soaring to 36 degrees. Chira's around 150 acres in size and 3,000 feet above sea level! The reservoir's stock of carp is relatively unknown; however there are thousands and thousands of carp between 20lb and a reservoir record of just over 50lb.

Scott and Simon got off to a brilliant start with Scott's first fish being a new PB of 35lb! The action was hectic all week with regular action early morning, afternoon, evening and right through the night. One night, 13 fish were caught and with having to continually reposition their rods at ranges of up to 150 meters by boat, next to no sleep was achieved.

The pair finished the week with 41 fish including fifteen 30s, one 41lb and the rest ranging between 19 and 29lb. All the fish were caught over beds of particles that I specially make up using a number of different ingredients and hookbaits consisting of tiger nuts; all of which were carefully prepared to give maximum leakage of the natural oils and flavours. Rigs were kept nice and simple with strong shockleaders, lead clips, braided hooklinks with a simple knotless knot setup and a size 6 hook.

The team at Canary Island Carp Fishing Tours can accommodate every angler's needs, from afternoon sessions to week-long carp fishing trips, sea fishing days, fly fishing for the huge population of black bass and even helicopter excursions to and from the reservoirs. Scott was certainly a happy customer. He said goodbye before adding, "It's the best fishing holiday I've ever had and we'll definitely be coming back!"

Dave Beecham — For more details of fishing trips/ holidays in Gran Canaria go to <u>www.carpgrancanaria. com</u> or telephone 0034 637 93 96 80

CENTRAL GRAN CANARIA

Green and Pleasant Land

If you've never smelt fresh pine before, and even if you have, the centre of the island is a must-visit. There's the beautifully-preserved *Pinar de Tamadaba*, the island's largest pine forest, to explore. The *caminos reales* here draw hikers and mountain-bikers like nectar attracts busy bees.

The rock-climbing fraternity also go over the top about Central GC. The *Pico de las Nieves* (Peak of the Snows), at 1,949 metres tall, is the highest point of the island. The area's also known as *Pozo de las Nieves* (Well of the Snows) because there's a well here that once collected snow which was used to conserve food in.

But it's not all countryside. Some of Gran Canaria's most attractive urban areas can be found here. Property prices reflect that with Monte Lentiscal very much Gran Canaria's stockbroker's belt.

Artenara

I'd wanted to visit Artenara ever since learning about it not long after relocating here. I'd none-too-subtly coughed it into conversations with my wife, the driver of the family. Also, I'd plead for the kids to tell their mother their father wished to go to Artenara for his birthday.

As a non-motorist, I didn't fancy the mammoth bus journey to the most isolated of Canarian communities. In the end, it was an in-flight magazine who put me out of my misery by commissioning me to write a feature about hiking in the area. And so I bagged a lift from old grey Las Palmas with Marcos the photographer.

Located just shy of 60km north of the *Playa del Inglés* lies the self-proclaimed *Cumbre de la Naturaleza* (Nature's Summit). Although, given the contrast between the desert-dry PDI and the verdant Artenara, you'd assume you were in another time zone altogether. One of the first things you'll notice is a bonsai version of Rio de Janeiro's legendary art-deco Christ statue overlooking the village. Nonetheless, it's still tall enough to dwarf the sightseers gathering below and make those of a paranoid persuasion even twitchier.

Beaches

Most of Artenara is non-coastal but there's a small accessible-by-walking-only area called *Punta Gongora* or *Punta de Las Arenas* (Sandy Point). Appealing to the traveller who subscribes to the going nowhere fast approach, the wind whips up fearsome waves. It also seems to have blown off all the clothing of the people on the beach. Yes, it's another nudist-friendly *playa*.

Food

Despite criticisms the waiting staff are actually attending tables in a parallel universe to your own, the state-run *Restaurante El Mirador de la Silla* (*Camino de la Silla* 9; 928 66 62 08) demands a visit. Enter the cave and make your way through an unlit tunnel which 60 metres later opens out into a beautiful sun terrace. Allegedly boasting the toilets with the best vistas in the world, they're certainly (rest) rooms with a view.

Accommodation

Self-catering is the name of the game in Artenara. Live like Barney, Wilma and co with a stay at one of Artenara's cave houses (686 795 849; www.artenatur.com). Yet with 21st-century home comforts including heating, it's not a total regression to the Stone Age.

Nightlife

You're. Having. A. Laugh.

Fiestas

The *Ermita de la Virgen de La Cuevita* is a hermitage dug into a cliff face 400 metres above the village centre. Every August 15th as part of the *Bajada de la Imagen* (Descent of the Statue) a procession leaves from here to *Iglesia de San Matías*, Artenara's parish church. The statue then returns to the chapel at nightfall, accompanied by bonfires and fireworks. The Artenara night is also lit up in Easter with the *Quema de Judas* (Burning of Judas), the biblical figure who assumes a Guy-Fawkes-style fall-guy.

Attractions

Sample the distinctive *pan de papas* (potato bread), a local delicacy, at the baker's *Panaderia Artenara* ((*Camino de la Silla* 1; 928 66 65 36) – the perfect fuel for exploring the area on foot. The municipality provides direct access to both the *Roque Nublo* and *Tamadaba* natural parks, with an extensive network of well-signposted hiking routes.

Santa Brigida

Travelling to the interior of the island through Monte Lentiscal feels like you're being transported to Switzerland with this Santa Brigida suburb resembling an upmarket Alpine resort, *sans* snow. The centre of Santa Brigida is similarly moneyed, enjoying a status as a popular base for Las Palmas' higher earners to commute from. I once attended a birthday party at a Santa Brigida residence whose owner not only had a garden on her land but caves too.

Santa Brigida also boasts one of the best *polideportivos* (sports centres) on the island. Many's a Sunday I've travelled there to play 5-a-side-football before hitting the swimming pool and spa afterwards. The weekend's end needn't be a day of rest, after all.

The municipality features a number of routes for cyclists and hikers to explore the rich natural beauty within sight, smell and sound. No wonder *Villa de Santa Brígida* describes itself as a *Paraiso Rural* (Rural Paradise). Where the Atlantic Ocean's an expanse of blue, the VDSB's a sea of green.

Beaches
Head to Las Palmas for your nearest shoreline.

Food
It's difficult to look beyond Monte Lentiscal if you're looking to get stuffed in Santa Brigida. The ever-inventive *Satautey* (*Calle de Real de Coello* 2; 828 01 04 21), the in-house restaurant of the *Hotel Escuela Santa Brigida*, trades in the established with a local twist, including ravioli stuffed with *gofio* rather than meat, octopus *tempura* coated in a batter of Canarian beer, and green, instead of the usual red, *gazpacho*. Nearby, the similarly adventurous *Restaurante Los Nacientes de Agua Dulce* (*Carretara General Centro* 116; 928 35 66 02) offers a modern take on traditional Canarian cooking.

Slightly further afield, heading up towards the neighbouring municipality of Vega de San Mateo, you'll come across

Restaurante Martell (*Carretara el Centro Madroñal KM 8; 928 64 12 83,*), which offers an unmissable culinary experience. I've yet to see a menu here and the eccentric owner will ensure you won't forget your meal in a hurry. I once asked for some *alioli* here but the owner refused, promising me something superior. True to his word, he brought what I can only describe as mushroom-infused olive oil, which tastes a whole lot better than it sounds. The kitchen source all the vegetables they use from the restaurant's own organic garden.

Accommodation

The four-star *Hotel Escuela Santa Brigida* (*Calle de Real de Coello* 2; 828 01 04 21) offers an education on how to run an establishment, to guests and its trainee hotel staff alike. *La Calzada* used to be a sleepy hamlet, before they built a *padel (*an Argentinian hybrid of squash and tennis) club there that puts the hoo into hooray henry. At the neighbouring *Hotel Rural Maipéz* (*Carretara de La Calzada* 104; 928 28 72 72; www.maipez.com), try and avoid the braying by concentrating on the excellent views of the emerald *Barranco de Guiniguada* below.

Nightlife

Las Palmas and its pulsating selection of bars and clubs is a mere 14km away from the main town of Santa Brígida.

Fiestas

Like the majority of the municipalities on the island, the biggest celebrations in *Villa de Santa Brígida* pay tribute to its patron saint. And so *Fiestas en Honor de Santa*

Brigida commemorate the life and times of good Saint Brigit on the first Saturday of August. Featuring the usual selection of floats and islanders dressed in traditional clothes, it's the busiest SB ever gets.

Attractions

For lovers of the outdoors, a walk through the *Barranco de Alonso* rewards you with a view of the bluff-hanging Dragon Tree – a beauty spot dating back half a Millennium. For craft enthusiasts, a trip to the *Ecomuseo Casa-Alfar Panchito* (*Camino de La Picota* 11; 928 28 82 70; <u>www.centrolocerolaatalaya.org</u>) in *La Atalaya* represents the chance to go beyond the keyhole of the cave house and workshop which belonged to master potter, Francisco Rodríguez Santana aka Panchito. The Santa Brigida native (1907-1986), a true country gent, was one of a long line of potters.

Tejeda

My wife surprised me with a lovely birthday treat a few years back with a stay at the then-recently reopened *Parador* in *Cruz de Tejeda*, one of a chain of state-run hotels with an excellent reputation. Recovering from a serious football-induced ankle injury, I was looking forward to rehabilitating in their spa – except it was closed because the water was considered to be too cold. My protestations that being English I didn't care fell on decidedly stony ground and I had to make do with sunning sessions on the surprisingly tropical terrace – it was April at the time.

I've been back to Tejeda since. It's a fantastic hiking area and my recovered ankle stood up to some serious pounding as I followed trails like the kid who used to spend his Christmas holidays exploring the part of Epping Forest which bordered his grandparents' house. Beginners can try their luck with a leisurely downwards sashay to nearby Teror.

A 44km drive from Las Palmas along a spiral of a road, the *Carretara del Centro*, Tejeda the town is further inland than Santa Brigida and Vega de San Mateo. The adjoining *Cruz de Tejeda*, a sizeable and solemn crucifix carved out of more-grey-than-green stone marks the once-imagined-to-be centre of the island. The scenery of this region is certainly dramatic with poet Miguel de Unamuno moved to describe the 18km-wide crater of *Caldera de Tejeda* as "a tremendous upset of the innards of the earth."

Beaches
With the abundant flora on show, you're more likely to see beeches than beaches in Tejeda.

Food
The fruits of the region's ubiquitous almond trees turn up in locally-made sweets including *bienmesabe* and *marzipan*. Those with more of a savoury tooth are directed to sample the Tejeda speciality of *potaje de jaramago* (rocket stew). A childhood haunt of my wife, *Asador Grill de Yolanda* (*Cruz de Tejeda S/N*; 928 66 62 76; www.asadoryolanda.com), whose tables spill out onto the pavement, specializes in meat and a few veg. The

owner must have been delighted when my wife and family pitched up, seeing as they numbered into double figures. The similarly omnivore-friendly *Restaurante Grill La Cumbre* (*Lugar Llano de la Pez S/N;* 928 17 00 69) is the place to go for good food simply done.

Accommodation

Alfonso XIII set up the *Paradores de Turismo de España* back in 1928, to promote Spanish tourism. Usually located in historic buildings such as castles and palaces, they've become a benchmark in luxury hotels. The *Parador de Cruz de Tejeda* (*Cruz de Tejeda S/N;* 928 01 25 00; www. parador.es) more than matches those high standards. In Tejeda Central, the three-star *Hotel Rural Fonda de la Tea* (*Calle Ezequiel Sánchez* 22; 928 66 64 22; www. hotelfondadelatea.com) reopened in 2007 after being closed for nigh on 50 years. Whilst its stone exterior and wooden balconies link to its past, the hotel provide 21st century comforts by way of their flat-screen TVs and Internet connections.

Nightlife

The only ambient music you'll hear in Tejeda will be on the speakers of the Café Lounge at *Let Me Take U* (629 19 86 85; www.letmetakeu.com) For an even later night, the owners organize guided tours of Las Palmas with pick-up from your hotel included. Bear in mind, though, that the venues you're likely to be taken to are gay-friendly ones.

Fiestas

As deeply religious as their counterparts in other Gran Canaria municipalities, the *Fiestas de la Virgen del Socorro*, which begin in the second week of September, see locals bring offerings to the patron saint at Tejeda's parish church. Rather more secular are the *Fiestas del Almendro en Flor* held during the first two weeks of February. These date back as recently as 1970 but nevertheless celebrate the history of the area, namely its almond trees.

Attractions

The *Museo de Abraham Cárdenes* (*Calle Leocadio Cabrera S/N*; 928 66 61 89) is a Tejeda museum which showcases the work of this local sculptor. Non-sculpted forms to look out for are the postcard-profilic *Roque Nublo* alongside the no-less-spectacular *Roque Bentayga*. Rock on, indeed. Phone in advance for a guided tour of the stunningly-set *Bodegas Bentayga* (Calle El Alberconcillo S/N; 928 42 60 47; www.bodegasbentayga.com). I've visisted Lanzarote's amazing *La Geria* wine region and for sheer suspension of belief, the 12 hectares of *BB* more than matches those volcanic vineyards.

Valleseco

Although their sense of humour, in common with the Spanish mainland, is very much a physical one (the theme tune to *Benny Hill* seems to be the mobile tone setting of choice) the Canarians do get irony. How else do you explain this municipality being called *Dry Valley*? When it has the highest annual rainfall of the entire island?

The town itself is, depending on your perspective, pretty/ pretty dull. What is beyond dispute is that it won't detain you for long. Its surroundings will, however, with the *caminos reales* providing a network of hiking trails to trek.

Very much a rural retreat, Valleseco's an area the local tourist board is keen to attract eco travellers to. They can't but help come away impressed if they hike the *Barranco de la Virgen*. Heading from the municipal capital to *Las Madres* by way of Valsendro, you'll walk through both pine and laurel forests whilst blue tits and kestrels flit and soar in the sky above.

Beaches
As wet as the Atlantic Ocean itself at times, nevertheless Valleseco doesn't do beaches.

Food
Where *Hermanos Garcia* do reasonably-priced yet bog-standard home cooking, *Hermanos Rogelio* organize

regular culinary events and co-operate with the likes of *Hecansa* to promote Gran Canaria as a gourmet location. I've had many bad meals in *Hermanos Garcia* from tuna turning up in my mixed salad despite my express demand that I wanted it *sin atun* to being served a plate of completely macerated boiled vegetables. *Hermanos Rogelio*, on the other hand, have never fallen below their exacting standards. And *Arcos de la Laguna* (*Cruce de La Laguna* S/N; 928 61 82 82) is *HR's* flagship restaurant, sourcing local ingredients and combining them to stylish and substantial effect.

Accommodation
80% of Valleseco's territory is protected with planning not merely restricted but banned outright. A perfect base for a hiking break, *Albergue Aula de la Laurisilva* (*Pico de Osorio* 22; 928 43 15 95; www.ludenatura.com) is a hostel set in Valleseco's self-styled Green Oasis. Part of the P*arque Rural de Doramas*, the *Casa de la Virgen* (*Barranco de la Virgen* 13; 630 07 46 13; www.casadelavirgen.com) along with the smaller *El Pajar*, a converted granary, enjoys 17,000 square metres of chestnut, fig and plum-tree foliage.

Nightlife
With eight high-quality hiking trails on your doorstep, you'll want to get your head down early in Valleseco. Thankfully, you don't have any other option given the moribund nocturnal scene. There are livelier cemetries.

Fiestas

The harvest festival of *Fiesta de la Manzana* held in the first week of October sees local farmers give up their apples as a tribute to *Nuestra Señora de la Encarnación* (Our Lady of the Incarnation). Fifty days after Easter Monday sometime in the Middle Ages, Dominican missionary San Vicente Ferrer (then plain Vince) left Teror to take up residence in Valleseco. And so the heavy-on-the-folklore *Fiestas de San Vicente*, depending on when Easter falls, take place in either May or June.

Attractions

Artisan Central, Valleseco boasts traditional craftsmen and women including carvers, sculptors, or weavers. For an introduction to their back catalogue, visit Valleseco's Tourist Information Office, *Oficina de Turismo de Valleseco* (*Calle León y Castillo* 27; 928 61 87 40) which finds room for a *Taller de Artesania*, Handicraft Workshop. Listen out for the pipes of peace at the *Iglesia de San Vicente Ferrer*. Emanating from an 18th-century organ which originally resided in Teror's church, they cast some spell. And watch maize being grinded into golden g*ofio* at the *Molino de Gofio* (Gofio Mill).

Vega de San Mateo

The Way to Saint Matthew – Vega de San Mateo

I initially thought there were two main settlements in this province: *Vega de San Mateo* (Way to Saint Matthew) and *San Mateo* (Saint Matthew). There's actually just one with the latter a shortcut of a name. How was I to know they meant 'way' in the spiritual sense of the word?

On my first-ever visit to Gran Canaria, my wife/then girlfriend took me to San Mateo. We still have a cheesy tourist photo of me posing next to the sign. And even after all these years, when I translate my name to Spanish, "*Mateo*" before adding "*San Mateo*" I never fail to provoke a giggle/resigned sigh.

I don't think I've played football in a stadium with better views than the one in *Vega de San Mateo*. Yet with the abundant surrounding greenery, I don't understand why they use an artificial pitch. Playing on real grass over here's the preserve of the professional footballer, it seems.

Beaches

With the exception of Artenara, there are no beaches in central Gran Canaria.

Food

Fidgety kids can gambol freely to and fro at *La Veguetilla* (*Avenida Tinamar 49;* 928 66 07 64; www. restaurantelaveguetilla.com), an establishment which thoughtfully includes a playground. A classy restaurant, the only gripe I have is that as a vegetarian the menu doesn't offer enough variety. It would be lovely for them to change it once in a while. Something which can also be said about *Área Recreativa El Calero* (*Calle La Lechucilla S/N;* 928 66 16 79) whose owner initially didn't understand what vegetarians were. She knocked up a mean egg and chips, though, a cut above transport-café standards. As much a picnic area as eatery, El Calero is a popular destination for families to spend quality time with each other of a Sunday.

Accommodation

In an article in *The Guardian*, they raved about La Lechuza, a tiny hamlet in Vega de San Mateo. The reaction of Ivan, one of my brother-in-law Victor's friends who owns a property close by, was an incredulous: "But there's nothing there." Make your own mind up with a stay at the hamlet's only hotel, the six-room *Hotel Rural Las Calas* (*Calle El Arenal* 36; 928 66 14 36; <u>www.hotelrurallascalas.com</u>). A manor house dating back to 1800, the warm, welcoming exterior's a toasted sunflower colour. A vegetarian menu here features vegetables grown in the hotel's own garden.

Nightlife

Time was when you could go to a nightclub in San Mateo and impress a local with the fact you were from Las Palmas. Friends of mine even went as far to use this as part of a chat-up routine. The world's a smaller place these days however, but you're more than welcome to give the tried-and-trusted line of "I'm from Las Palmas, don't you know?" a go.

Fiestas

The *Fiestas de San Mateo*, in homage to the munipality's patron saint, dominate the cultural calendar. As well as the usual pilgrimage, look out for the accompanying horse race and livestock fair. This party takes place on the 21st September every year.

Attractions

Supermarkets in Gran Canaria are far inferior to those elsewhere. However, greengrocers are a lot better and definitely more plentiful. But the best place to shop for fruit and veg are the markets, which are predominately covered rather than featuring stalls on the streets. And the pick of Gran Canaria's farmers' markets is undoubtedly the *Mercadillo de San Mateo*. Open on Sundays, take advantage of the free samples but if you don't want to cause offence, remember to buy as well as try.

For the love of God – Vega de San Mateo church

ESSENTIAL TRAVEL INFORMATION

> "The hotel's a bit odd, I've never seen as many cross-eyed people in one location."
> Karl Pilkington, Ricky Gervais's round-headed sidekick, recalls his Gran Canaria holiday

EMERGENCY TELEPHONE NUMBERS

If you only remember one phone number, remember 112. This is the EU number covering all your emergency needs. Call 112 for an ambulance, police, and fire services or mountain and sea rescue. Operators speak English and German as well as Spanish.

CRIME

In the Chelsea-Headhunters-glorifying *Football Factory*, they reveal the old football hooligan's trick of asking somebody the time. The thugs aren't interested in what you answer but how. As your reply would determine where you came from.

I fell foul of this particular scam on a walk home from a night out in Las Palmas when one of a group of non-hooded youths practically spat out the question: "*¿Que hora es?*" It was probably my delay in replying as much as my non-fluent Spanish that triggered his wild punch. Thankfully, he didn't really connect and I was able to escape. There you have it, my only experience of crime on the island.

On the whole, the island's relatively crime-free. Pickpocketing does go on, mainly in the southern resorts, so a money belt might be a better option than a purse or wallet. Dressing down rather than up is another way to avoid being used as a walking cashpoint.

"There's one car for every two people in Las Palmas, so it's impossible to find a parking space. Look for multi-storey car parks, where you may find a bay free. In our experience, parking in resorts is easier – although you do have to pay and display in the centre of most resorts. We found the traffic jams on the island horrendous, especially at weekends, when locals are heading to or from the beach. We would advise avoiding driving anywhere early in the morning and in the late afternoon, especially in the south-east of the island." Tourist Alan Docherty on Gran Canaria's motoring madness.

DRIVING

If you're old enough, you're good enough seems to be the mantra regarding driving on Gran Canaria. Everybody of legal age seems to have a licence. Yet their interpretation of safe driving is a rough and ready one with any dents on their motor worn like a badge of honour.

Drinking and driving is a sad fact of life over here. Indeed, in some of the poorer areas, the taxi rank is an unofficial one, situated outside the most popular bar. This is what you'd like the *Guardia Civil* to stamp down on, rather than their collaring of motorists for more innocuous offences that many believe are mere fundraising initiatives.

In common with mainland Europe, Canarians drive on the right-hand side of the road. So bear that in mind if you're thinking of renting a hire car. Most roads are well-maintained, however, if you're planning a Route-66-style tour of the island.

HEALTH

Gran Canaria's public health service is something you can rely on, although, given its popularity, waiting times are often long. As a Spanish province, the standard of care is equivalent to what you would expect on the mainland. It's free for anyone who pays Spanish insurance contributions or has a European Health Insurance Card (EHIC).

There are two public hospitals on Gran Canaria, both in Las Palmas. You'll spot the older one, *Complejo Hospitalario Universiario Insular Materno Infantil* (*Avenida Marítima del Sur S/N*; 928 44 40 00) on your drive from the airport to Las Palmas. The newer *Complejo Hospitalario Doctor Negrin* (*Plaza Barranco la Ballena S/N*; 928 45 00 00) lies closer to the GC-2 which connects LP with the north and west coasts of the island.

In the south of the island, *Hospital San Roque Maspalomas* (*Calle Mar de Siberia* 1; 928 06 36 00) is a public-private collaboration. Taking NHS referrals from the *centros de salud* (health centres), you'll receive free treatment if you have an EHIC or Spanish social security card. Alternatively, the British Medical Clinic in Puerto Rico (*Avenida Roca Bos*ch 4; 928 56 00 16; www.britishmedicalclinic.com) is a private medical practice offering services to non-Spanish speakers.

While the EHIC entitles you to free health care, it doesn't cover the cost of repatriation. In the event of a serious health issue, private insurance is required to foot the bill of transportation back to your home country. If your ailment is minor, a *farmacia* should be your first port of call.

SHOPPING

Best Buys

Boasting tax-free status, the Canaries are a destination of choice for bargain-hunters. Every major town and resort features a selection of cheap electronic and perfume shops. Meanwhile, lovers of cigarettes and alcohol should head to the island's supermarkets who stock local, national, and international brands at discount prices.

For a souvenir with a difference, you could always bring back some aloe vera, the island's mythical medicinal herb. You'll find aloe vera products in shops across the island, but for the best range, Las Palmas' *Aloe Vera Store Canarias* (*Calle Ripoche* 29, 928 26 43 03; www.aloestorecanarias.com). Although the jury's still out on their hair restorer.

Food

An intricate infrastructure of supermarkets serves the north of the island. Despite the pound and Euro now being of roughly equal value, weekly shopping bills are considerably less than you're used to. The cheapest supermarket *Mercadona* (but only if you buy their *Bosque Verde* and *Hacendado* brands) seems to sprout new branches on a regular basis. I've heard conflicting reports about the value for money offered by Basque budget supermarket chain *Eroski* who opened their first Canarian operation in Jinámar´s *Centro Comercial el Mirador* in 2010.

Other popular supermarkets include *Hiperdino* and *Spar*, but expect to pay more as they're usually located in the centre of town rather than the more out-of-the-way *Mercadona*. Even more expensive still are the *Carrefour* hypermarket and the supermarket within the *El Corte Ingles* deparment store. Yet the range of products is far wider here and you'll more likely to find stuff you're used to buying in your home country.

Supermarkets in the southern resorts exist for the benefit of tourists. A fact reflected in their higher prices and smaller sizes. Pickpockets are not the only threat to your wallet in the south.

For a real taste of Gran Canaria, check out their fruit and vegetables. Bananas, onions, tomatoes and watercress are all grown on the island. Yet while it's easy to buy local, you'll find that it's often more expensive as the supplier is a small producer. Cheese is another Canarian delicacy. You're be able to pick up the famous *quesos de flor* at supermarkets all over the island or in specialist shops within the regions it's mainly produced, namely Santa María de Guía and Valsequillo.

Clothes

On the high streets of Las Palmas and within the island's many, many, many shopping centres you'll find the Spanish trio of *Cortefiel*, *Springfield*, and *Zara*. More expensive imports include *Pepe Jeans* and *Levi's*. *El Corte Inglés* boasts brand-name fashion at cheaper prices than you'd imagine. Even more reasonable are their own collections: *Easy Wear* and *fórmul@ Joven*.

El Corte Inglés is also a good place for shoes, especially if you want a more personal service. Elsewhere, *Pablosky* seem to have a monopoly on children's shoes. For less petite feet, women can find footwear at *Carolina Boix*.

RESOURCES

WORKING

Adecco (*Calle Néstor de la Torre* 46, Las Palmas; 928 24 86 11; www.adecco.es) – Search and apply for jobs across all employment sectors in Las Palmas and beyond.

Manpower (*Calle León y Castillo* 431, Las Palmas; 928 26 90 51; www.manpower.es) – Browse mainly short-term vacancies and register as a jobseeker at this internationally-renowned firm.

Personal 7 (*Calle Plácido Domingo* 2, San Fernando; 928 77 49 54; www.grupoconstant.com/personal7) – Submit your CV with this agency if you're looking for a career in the service industry in the south of the island.

NETWORKING

Gran Canaria Noticeboard (www.facebook.com/grancanarianoticeboard) – Keep up to date with all the latest expat developments courtesy of the social network

The British Club (*Calle León y Castillo 274*; 928 24 31 59) – Don't forget your English at a member's club made up almost exclusively of British expats

Womens International Network Gran Canarian (womensnetwork@hotmail.es) – Email for further details about an established group of women who meet on the 8th of each month in Arguineguín combining business with pleasure.

MAGAZINES AND NEWSPAPERS

Canarias 7 (www.canarias7.es) and *La Provincia* (www.laprovincia.es)
Gran Canaria's two main daily Spanish-language newspapers. They're pretty similar, although I favour *Canarias 7* because I prefer their supplements. Handy for improving your Spanish they're also good to use as a what's on guide.

Coliseo (www.revistacoliseo.com)
Slim free bi-monthly publication in Spanish and (very formal) English which bills itself as *La Mejor Guía de Arte y Escena*/The Best Art and Scene Guide.

Island Connections (www.islandconnections.eu)
An established fortnightly English-language newspaper reporting on all of the seven Canary Islands, but with a heavy Tenerife bias.

La Bohemia (www.labohemia.es)
Ingeniously-designed cultural guide doubles as a listings mag for kids as you'll see when turning it over to reveal *La Peque Bohemia*.

The Canary News (www.thecanarynews.com)
The only English-language newspaper based on Gran Canaria also includes pages translated for the benefit of the south's Swedish expats.

BOOKS

Wild Flowers of the Canary Islands: David and Zoe Bramwell: ISBN: 978-0859502276

Medicinal Plants of the Canary Islands: David Bramwell: ISBN: 978-8472071728
It's a botanist's dream on Gran Canaria and these two illustrated books should take pride of place in your rucksack. David Bramwell has been director of Tafira Alta's acclaimed Jardín Botánico Canario since 1972.

Don't Leave Gran Canaria Without Seeing It – 25 Great Hikes: Roger Bradley
Kompass Map 0237: Gran Canaria:
ISBN: 978-3854911142
Rambling Roger showed me yet another side to Gran Canaria with an informative tour of Artenara and his book is an excellent resource covering the island's circular treks. He recommends the Kompass map as the best visual guide to walking in Gran Canaria.

WEBSITES

Active Canaria: www.activecanaria.com
The beach bum/couch-potato might not agree, but Gran Canaria boasts the perfect climate to run in the sun. Active Canaria offer orienteering training and maps for sale.

Canary Forum: www.canaryforum.com
A friendly online community which centres mainly on southern, and therefore British, concerns. A great place to meet and greet fellow expats, nonetheless.

Cycle Gran Canaria: www.cyclegrancanaria.com
Rent a bike to explore Las Palmas and beyond or join a tour. Ease your way into travelling the island by navigating LP's cycle paths before tackling the mountains above Maspalomas. If you dare.

GranCanaria: www.grancanaria.com
You'd expect the official tourist board's site to be stylish (which it is) but it's also substantial. View an exhaustive calendar and overview of the island's municipalities in English, Dutch, French, German, Portuguese, Polish, Spanish, and Swedish.

Gran Canaria Guru: www.grancanariaguru.com
Sadly, it's not as refreshed as it once was, nevertheless GCG remains an invaluable source of hints and tips for those looking to live and work on the island.

Gran Canaria Info: www.gran-canaria-info.com
Lex Thoonen is a rare expat in that he's chosen to settle in the western outpost of Agaete but his site focuses on the south of the island, offering a portal that's of use to residents and tourists alike.

Hollandse Nieuwe: www.hollandsenieuwe.com
Dutch resource also caters for Belgians who have relocated to Gran Canaria.

Rambling Roger's Hiking Routes: www.ramblingroger.com
Were your boots made for walking? If so, let Roger and Eileen Bradley tell you all about the excellent terrain you'll be able to explore on Gran Canaria.

Sunshine Guide to Gran Canaria: http://www.alexbramwell.blogspot.com
Freelance photographer and writer Alex Bramwell, Las Palmas born and bred, offers fascinating recommendations for active sorts in Gran Canaria. As you'd expect, the site is beautifully illustrated with first-rate photography.

The Cunning Canary: www.cunningcanary.com
Freelance writer and expat Victoria Smith keeps her entertaining and opinionated blog up to date with news and views, and offers invaluable advice when she replies to any queries.

MORE LINKS

If you know the name of the business you're trying to locate or want to browse hotels or restaurants, you can't go far wrong by flicking through good old Yellow Pages: www.paginasamarillas.es

It's no longer compulsory for you to register at either the British (Calle Luis Morote 6, 3rd Floor, Las Palmas; 902 109 356) or Irish Consulate (Calle León y Castillo 195, 1st Floor, Las Palmas; 928 29 77 28). However, they're as useful in helping expats settle as aiding tourists in distress. All members of staff are English-speaking.

ABOUT THE AUTHOR

In 2004 Matthew Hirtes was working at SkySports Centre as a subtitler. His work colleagues, looking out at another grey Isleworth day, couldn't believe his luck when he told them he was leaving to start a new life with his Canarian wife Cristina and two boys Alex and Dani in Las Palmas. Imagining one long version of Wham's *Club Tropicana* video. On repeat. Until Matthew alerted them to the BBC weather site which showed that just as in west London, it was raining too in Las Palmas.

Based in the north of the island, they now live in a central Las Palmas flat within walking distance of their English language academy and their children's school. Matthew combines teaching by day with parenting and writing in the evenings and weekends. He's also a keen football dad and still plays for a team himself.

A former Las Palmas correspondent for *RTN Canarias*, Matthew now writes features about the Canaries for the likes of *Condé Nast Traveller* and *The Independent*. A one-time deputy editor of *The Official Chelsea Magazine*, he also contributes articles to *Sports Illustrated*. His freelance work has taken him to places few residents let alone tourists ever see.

What Matthew has discovered is an island whose rich and varied geography and history remains a mystery to many. Truly, there is life beyond the bucket and spade. You can count the major resorts on one hand but you'd need a calculator to detail what the rest of the island has to offer.

A veteran expat, Matthew has written *Going Local in Gran Canaria* so that more inquisitive visitors and open-minded new residents can truly grasp what this mini-continent has to show for itself. Having typed over 40,000 words however, his fingers need a rest. It's time for his feet to do some work again.

INDEX

Barranco de Guayadeque 125
Barranco de la Mina 81
Barranco de la Virgen 116
Barranco de los Cernícalos 136,
Basilica de Nuestra Señora del Pino (Teror) 76, 121,
Basilica de San Juan Bautista (Telde) 131, 133
Bradley, Roger (aka Rambling Roger) 68-69, 210-11
Bramwell, David 79-80, 210
Buses 33-34, 59

C

CAAM (*Centro Atlántico de Arte Moderno*) 110
Cactualdea 175
Caldera de Bandama 79
Caldera de Tejeda 192
Calderas 68
Camel rides 73
Caminos reales 185, 195
Camping 174
Canarias Jazz & Más 89-90
Carnaval 21-22, 25, 69, 75, 89, 110, 144
Casa Brito (restaurant) 94
Casa de Colón (museum) 6, 111
Casa de la Virgen (rural house) 196
Casa de los Camellos (hotel) 126
Casa de los Patrones de la Virgen (museum) 123
Casa de los Quintana 119
Casa-Museo Tomás Morales 114
Casa Rural Cercado de Don Paco 159
Casa Rural de Drago 113
Casa Rural Doña Margarita 122

H

NativeSpain.com

Going Native in
Tenerife

Andrea & Jack Montgomery

the essential guide to making yourself at home

How to Buy
SPANISH PROPERTY
and Move to
SPAIN

SAFELY

NICK SNELLING